CONTENTS

NOTES

3.2.1 Exercise Physiology

What students need to learn			Yes	Nearly	No
3.2.1.1: Diet and nutrition and their effect on physical activity and performance	Understand the exercise-related function of food classes.	Carbohydrate.			
		Fibre.			
		Fat (saturated fat, trans fat and cholesterol).			
		Protein,			
		Vitamins (C, D, B-12, B-complex),			
		Minerals (sodium, iron, calcium).			
		Water (hydration before, during and after physical activity).			
	Positive and negative effects of dietary supplements/manipulation on the performer.	Creatine, sodium bicarbonate, caffeine, Glycogen loading.			
3.2.1.2: Preparation and training methods in relation to	Understanding of the key terms relating to laboratory conditions and field tests.	Quantitative and qualitative.			
		Objective and subjective.			

maintaining physical activity and performance		Validity and reliability.			
	Physiological effects and benefits of a warm-up and cool down.	Stretching for different types of physical activity (static and ballistic).			
	Principles of training.	Specificity, progressive overload, reversibility, recovery, Frequency, Intensity Time, Type of Training (FITT) principles.			
	Application of principles of periodisation.	Macro cycle, Meso cycle, Micro cycle. Preparation, competition, transition. Tapering, peaking.			
	Training methods to improve physical fitness and health.	HIIT/interval training (anaerobic power). Continuous training (aerobic power). Fartlek (aerobic power). Circuit training (muscular endurance).			

		Weight training (strength). Proprioceptive Neuromuscular Facilitation (PNF) (flexibility).			
3.2.1.3: Injury prevention and the rehabilitation of injury	Types of injury.	Acute (fractures, dislocations, strains, sprains). Chronic (achilles tendonitis, stress fracture, 'tennis elbow').			
	Understanding different methods used in injury prevention, rehabilitation and recovery.	Injury prevention methods: Screening. Protective equipment. Warm up, flexibility training (active, passive, static and ballistic), taping and bracing. Injury rehabilitation methods (proprioceptive training, strength			

		training, hyperbaric chambers, cryotherapy, hydrotherapy). Recovery from exercise (compression garments, massage/foam rollers, cold therapy, ice bath, cryotherapy).			
	Physiological reasons for methods used in injury rehabilitation.	Hyperbaric chambers, cryotherapy.			
	Importance of sleep and nutrition for improved recovery.				

4

THE EXERCISE RELATED FUNCTION OF FOOD

- PROTEIN (macronutrient)
- VITAMINS (micronutrient)
- MINERALS (micronutrient)
- FIBRE (it is a macronutrient in terms of it is needed in large amounts, but it does not provide energy).
- WATER (as with fibre, water is a macronutrient in the sense it is needed in large amounts, but it does not provide energy).

There are 7 elements of nutrition that should be included in a balanced diet & these are...

- CARBOHYDRATES (macronutrient)
- FATS (macronutrient)

MICRONUTRIENTS
- Are required in smaller amounts.
- They are not energy providers
- Aid essential body functions - growth, development & general health.

Breakdown of Calorific Intake
- 45 - 65 % from carbohydrates
- 20 - 35% from fats
- 10 - 25% from protein.

A BALANCED DIET
- Is essential for healthy body function, as well as meeting the nutritional requirements for everyday living.
- For a performer it is even more imperative to keep the body healthy for the rigours of regular intense training, whether that be for fuel or fuel replenishment, or for growth and repair of muscle tissue.

MACRONUTRIENTS
- Are required in large amounts.
- Provide the body with energy.
- The 'generic' percentage range of macronutrients required in the diet is outlined to the right.
- However, these will vary depending on how much energy the performer uses, body type and the type of activity participated in. eg. power, endurance etc.

THE EXERCISE RELATED FUNCTION OF FOOD II

CARBOHYDRATES

- Comprises of sugar molecules (saccharides), which contain carbon, hydrogen & oxygen.
- Are the main nutrient required for energy in the body, especially for high intensity exercise.
- If not enough carbohydrates are consumed, the body will use protein & fats as an energy source, which is not always ideal (especially protein as the major fuel source).
- Carbohydrates break down into glucose which travels into the bloodstream (plasma), into the body's cells with the help of the hormone insulin.
- It is stored as glycogen in muscles & the liver.
- Carbohydrates can be divided into 2 categories based on how many sugar molecules they contain.
  - Simple (sugar)
  - complex (starch).

SIMPLE (SUGAR)

- Contain 1 or 2 sugar molecules & include glucose, fructose, sucrose & lactose.
- Generally have a higher glycaemic index (high GI), released into the bloodstream at a quicker rate.
- Simple carbohydrates should be consumed as a lower percentage compared to complex carbohydrates, as they are often consumed from refined foods (processed + fibre & minerals removed).
- eg. cakes, sweets, breakfast cereals (processed)
- healthier simple carbohydrates include fruit, fruit juices & milk products.

COMPLEX (STARCH)

- Contain more complex chains of sugars, such as polysaccharides. Also contain fibre.
- Generally have a lower glycaemic index (low GI), released into the bloodstream at a slower rate.
- Should be the main staple of carbohydrates eaten.
- Include foods such as whole grains (brown bread, rice, pasta & cereals, sweet potatoes, peas, beans & fruit.

FIBRE

- Essential. Cannot be made by the body.
- Found in fruit, vegetables, legumes, seeds, nuts & whole grains.
- Most fibre is insoluble (not digested) Helps with healthy digestion & elimination of waste.
- Soluble fibre consumed in small amounts. Regulates blood sugar levels & lowers cholesterol.

THE EXERCISE RELATED FUNCTION OF FOOD III

PROTEIN

- Protein should not be the major source of energy, as its major role revolves around being the 'building blocks' of the body.

- However, it does contribute to the energy pathways in smaller percentages.

- Consists of amino acids & are important for muscle growth & repair & the formation of enzymes, hormones & haemoglobin.

- food sources that provide higher levels of protein include meat, fish & dairy products.

- A healthier fat source comes from unsaturated fats that are generally associated with a Mediterranean diet.

- eg. olive & canola oils, avacados, nuts (pecans, almonds, hazlenuts) & seeds (pumpkin and sesame).

FATS

- Are essential for lubricating joints, helping organs produce hormones, allow the body to absorb certain vitamins (A, D, E & K), reduce inflammation & be a major provider of energy.

- Fat has a higher energy yield than carbohydrates. However, approximately 15% of energy needs to be consumed to utilise fat in the aerobic pathway.

- This is something 'more conditioned' performers can do.

- Saturated fat mainy comes from animal sources & can lead to weight gain, CHD, diabetes & hypertension if consumed in large quantities over a prolonged period of time.

- Trans fats include unsaturated fats that have been processed with hydrogen & vegetable oils which cause the oil to become solid at room temperature.

- This type of fat can be found in meat & dairy products, but can lead to high levels of blood cholesterol (LDL).

THE EXERCISE RELATED FUNCTION OF FOOD IV

WATER

- Hydration is vital in sport, before, during & after physical activity.
- An adult is made up of approximately 60% water.

- Therefore water is essential not just for performance, but to survive!
- It is recommended that individuals consume 2 litres or 8 glasses of water per day, though other sources can come from fruit & vegetables.
- It is important to maintain hydration before, during & after exercise for the following reasons...

- Blood viscosity - dehydration leads to blood becoming too viscous. Maintaining viscosity levels allows plasma to stay at the right levels & transport important hormones, nutrients & RBCs to the muscles.
- Reduces fatigue & the effects of dehydration. eg dizziness, headaches.
- Maintain healthy HR range (an increase in viscosity leads to an increase in SV).
- To maintain optimal performance.

VITAMINS

- There are 13 vitamins in total, with 8 coming from the B group vitamins which are needed in small amounts.

- There are fat soluble vitamins, found in dairy, vegetable oils & oily fish.
- They are stored in the liver & fat tissue.

- Water soluble vitamins are also found in dairy, but are also abundant in fruit and vegetables.
- They are not stored & as such should be consumed on a daily basis.
- Food sources & benefits to the performer can be seen on the table on the next page.

- The body does not make minerals, therefore diet is important to maintain the correct levels in the body.

MINERALS

- Are small molecules that usually enter the body in combination with another atom & assist in a variety of bodily functions.
- Are dissolved in the body as ions (or electrolytes).

UITAMINS

Vitamin	Food source	Benefit to a sportsperson
C (ascorbic acid)	Fruits (especially citric fruits) and vegetables (particularly green vegetables).	• Antioxidant that destroy free radicals to protect the cells. • Fight infection by keeping the body healthy • Assists iron absorption • Collagen formation - strengthening bones, teeth, skin, blood vessels and ligaments
D	Exposure to sunlight. Small amounts (5-10%) from oily fish (salmon) and eggs.	Important for strong bones by helping to absorb calcium, muscles and overall health.
B-12	Clams, beef liver, fortified yeasts, plant milks, and breakfast cereals, some oily fish.	To help make red blood cells, maintain metabolism and the health of the nervous system.
B-Complex	These vitamins help our bodies use the macronutrients for fuel and some B-group vitamins are needed to help cells to multiply by making new DNA, except for B-12 and folate (B9) which are stored by the liver. • B1 (thiamin) works with the B group vitamins which helps to breakdown and release energy from food and helps to keep the nervous system healthy. • B2 (riboflavin) works with other B group vitamins works similar to B1, however it also helps to maintain healthy skin, eyes and the nervous system. • B6 assists in the formation of haemoglobin and to use the stored energy from carbohydrates and protein. Foods where the vitamin B-complex can be found include, meat, fish, dairy, nuts, cereals, fruit and vegetables.	

MINERALS

Mineral	Food source	Benefit to a sportsperson
Sodium	• Salt • Wholegrains • Meat • Dairy products • Highly processed foods	• Helps to maintain the correct volume of circulating blood and tissue fluids in the body. • Helps with transmission of nervous impulses into the muscle fibre.
Iron	Iron can be found in animal and plant foods including: • red meat and offal • fish • poultry • legumes • eggs • breakfast cereals with added iron.	• Transport of oxygen in the blood (needed to help form haemoglobin) • Help the immune system function effectively to fight infection.
Calcium	Dairy foods like milk, yoghurt and cheese and some plant-based foods with added calcium like soymilk, tofu, kale, broccoli and parsley.	• Strengthen bones and teeth • Regulate muscle and heart function • Blood clotting • Transmission of nervous system messages • Enzyme function.

ELECTROLYTE SOLUTIONS

OSMOLALITY

Refers to the concentration of dissolved particles of chemicals & minerals/electrolytes (eg Mg++) in a fluid.

Higher osmolality means _more_ particles in the fluid (hypertonic) & lower osmolality means they are more diluted (hypotonic).

ELECTROLYTES

Are minerals that dissolve in a fluid creating positive or negative ions used in various metabolic roles/processes.

They are important for proper nerve & muscle function, maintaining pH levels & hydration.

Electrolytes are lost through respiration (sweating).

Examples of electrolytes essential for muscle contractions in the body are;

- SODIUM (Na+) involved in muscle excitability & cellular permeability.

- POTASSIUM (K+) involved in protein & CHO synthesis.

- CALCIUM (Ca++ or Ca2+) involved in muscle contraction within myofibril.

- MAGNESIUM (Mg+) involved in the proper functioning of the Na+/K+ - ATPase pump & helps maintain Ca++ homeostasis.

Plus... CHLORIDE, PHOSPHATE & BICARBONATE.

HYPERTONIC

Have a higher osmolality than the body (more than 10% CHO). It supplements CHO or used post-exercise, especially when the activity is high intensity or long duration. Should be consumed/taken with HYPOTONIC solutions to reduce dehydration levels.

eg marathon runner.

ISOTONIC

Have a similar osmolality as the body (6-8% CHO). These drinks quickly replace lost fluids & glucose.

Most sports drinks are isotonic.

eg Lucozade Sport, Powerade & Gatorade.

They are the preferred solution during exercise, sport or game.

eg football, netball, rugby.

HYPOTONIC

Lower osmolality than the body (2-4% CHO).

Quickly replaces fluids & less CHO replacement.

Good for short duration activities. eg gymnastics & sprinting.

11

SUPPLEMENTS

BEETROOT JUICE

Drinking beetroot juice raises nitric oxide levels in the blood. This helps to promote vasodilation of blood vessels, leading to increased blood flow & O_2 to working muscles.

It also decreases the effects of DOMS & so is used post performance.

CHERRY JUICE

Tart cherry juice has an antioxidant & anti-inflammatory properties.

It can decrease pain & accelerate recovery after exercise. Useful for both strength & endurance events.

Can cause bloating & weight gain, so practise in training.

CAFFEINE

Is a stimulant. Increases mental alertness. It increases the breakdown of fat stores for energy, therefore decreasing the use of glycogen stores. Reduces fatigue for aerobic events (eg. marathon). However, excess caffeine can act as a diuretic & increase dehydration. Can also increase anxiety levels.

CREATINE MONOHYDRATE

Creatine loading is used to increase the PC stores in the muscles, thereby enhancing the replenishment of ATP.

This in turn helps to decrease recovery time & allows performers to participate in high intensity sports with greater levels of force & intensity. eg. power based sports, including; sprinting, rugby, weightlifting & basketball.

This procedure can/could potentially lead to bloating, water retention & long term kidney damage, though the evidence is inconclusive.

CARBOHYDRATE LOADING

- A method that is used prior to exercise / performance, leading up to an event to maximise glycogen stores. Usually a 10 day programme.
- High intense training for 6-7 days prior to event to deplete glycogen stores.
- Diet high in fat & protein initially & low in CHO.
- Increase CHO intake 3-4 days prior to competition as well as tapering training intensity & levels of fat & protein intake.
- Result → high levels of loading & storage of muscle & liver glycogen stores.
- Assists with endurance based events eg. marathon.

SODIUM BICARBONATE

Buffers the build up of lactate & H+, reducing blood acidity.

Allows the performer to work at a higher level of intensity, for longer without suffering the effects of fatigue. Can cause stomach cramps & nausea. eg. 400m sprinter (runner).

UNDERSTANDING KEY TERMS RELATING TO LABORATORY CONDITIONS & FIELD TESTS

OBJECTIVE & SUBJECTIVE

- Objective data involves facts & figures and is easily measurable.
- eg- the multi-stage Fitness Test.
- factual data is used to measure the aerobic fitness levels of a performer.

- Subjective data is based on opinions & interpretations.
- eg- in boxing, there is a generic criterion about a performance, but judges make a subjective account for the performance of the 2 boxers when giving a decision based on the scoring points system based on their own opinions and interpretation.

QUANTITATIVE & QUALITATIVE

- Quantitative data is anything that can be counted or measured with the use of data
- eg- using the data from various fitness tests gives a value to make a judgement based on the scores.
- Qualitative data is descriptive, referring to 'things' that can be observed & is subjective.
- eg- the Borg Scale (RPE) is a qualitative method where participants make a subjective judgement based on how hard they think they are working.
- Quantitative & qualitative analysis procedures are quite often used together.

- Occurs when data is analysed & judgements made based on the data.
- Often occurs when analysing strengths & weaknesses after a battery of fitness tests, to decide the best aims needed for a training programme.

RELIABILITY

- Refers to whether the results are consistent and reproducible over time & whether the procedures can be followed precisely during each repeated test.

- There are specific factors to consider, including...

  - Calibration of equipment.

  - Human error v technological assistance (time keeping v touch pads or timing gates).

  - Warm up.

UNDERSTANDING KEY TERMS RELATING TO LABORATORY CONDITIONS & FIELD TESTS II

- Correct technique

- Number of attempts

- Recovery time

- consistency between attempts.

- Instructions for the tests being accurately followed.

Focus On...
- Quantitative.
- Qualitative.
- subjective.
- objective.

- Reliability.
- Validity.

VALIDITY & RELIABILITY

VALIDITY

- Must ensure that the test actually evaluates the component of fitness that has been chosen, as well as ensuring that it is specific to the chosen sport/activity.

- eg. the 30m sprint test would be valid for testing speed. However, it would be invalid if it was used to test speed for a netball player/performer.

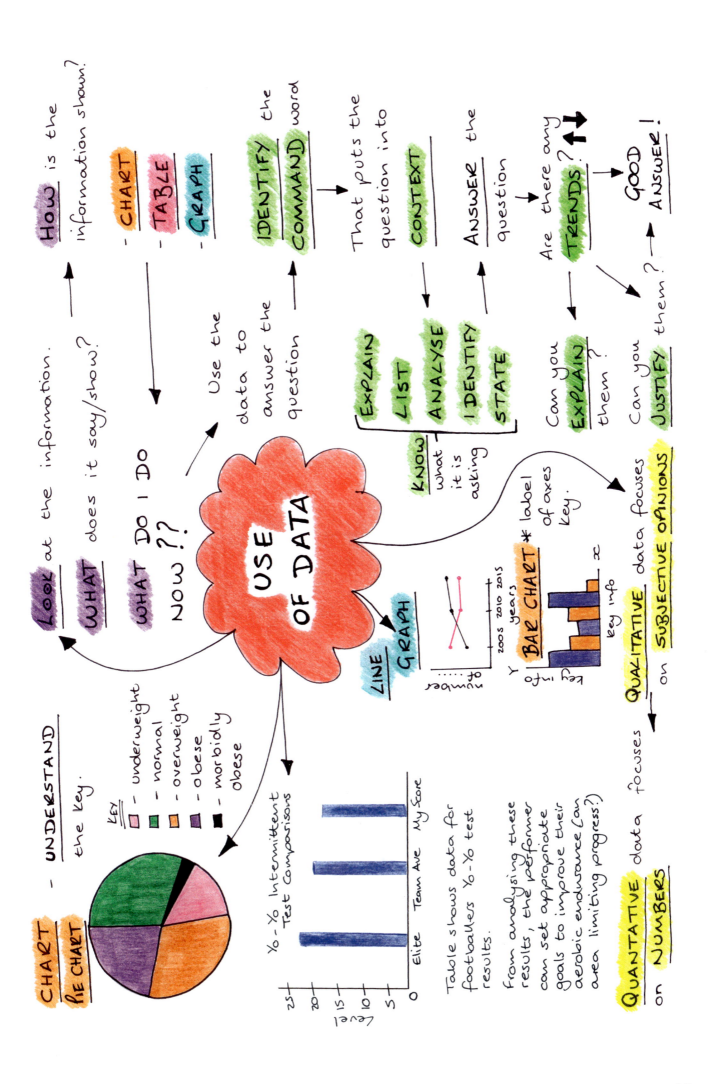

How is the information shown?

- **CHART**
- **TABLE**
- **GRAPH**

IDENTIFY the **COMMAND** word → That puts the question into **CONTEXT**

ANSWER the question → Are there any **TRENDS**? → **GOOD ANSWER**!

Can you **EXPLAIN** them?

Can you **JUSTIFY** them?

EXPLAIN
LIST
ANALYSE
IDENTIFY
STATE

KNOW what it is asking

Look at the information. What does it say/show?

WHAT DO I DO NOW??!

Use the data to answer the question

USE OF DATA

LINE GRAPH

2005 2010 2015
years
number to number

BAR CHART * label of axes / key.
Y
key info
key info
x

QUALITATIVE data focuses on **SUBJECTIVE OPINIONS**

QUANTITATIVE data focuses on **NUMBERS**

CHART - UNDERSTAND the key.

KEY
- underweight
- normal
- overweight
- obese
- morbidly obese

CHART - PIE CHART

Yo-Yo Intermittent Test Comparisons

25
20
15
10
5
0
Level
Elite   Team Ave   My Score

Table shows data for footballers Yo-Yo test results.

From analysing these results, the performer can set appropriate goals to improve their aerobic endurance (an area limiting progress?)

15

PHYSIOLOGICAL EFFECTS AND BENEFITS OF A WARM UP AND COOL DOWN

WARM UP

- Increases body temperature, leading to greater speed & force of muscle contraction due to an increase in enzyme output.
- There is an increase in enzyme activity.
- An increase in body temperature will also lead to greater muscle pliability.
- Increases the rate at which gaseous exchange occurs, allowing the body to prepare for the upcoming activity.
- Greater rate of O_2 delivery & CO_2 dispersal.
- Increased secretion of synovial fluid, making joints move with more fluency.
- Vascular shunting to help direct O_2 rich blood to areas of need.

- A WARM UP occurs prior/before the activity takes place.
- A COOL DOWN occurs after the activity has taken place.

COOLING DOWN

An active cooldown is more effective for promoting post-exercise recovery than a passive cool down involving no activity.

It helps accelerate dispersion of lactate in blood, recovery of pH to resting levels, recovery of Cardiovascular & Respiratory systems & reduce the effects of DOMS.

It should involve low/moderate aerobic element + static stretches. (benefits not fully conclusive).

- Priming: a way of manipulating the warm up to accelerate O_2 uptake, maximising the use of the aerobic pathway as the main energy system, as this is more efficient, with less inhibiting factors to consider.

- Reduces the chance of injury (although contradictory & inconclusive) Does a warm up reduce the risk of concussion?
- Psychological benefits also help reduce anxiety & get the performer 'in the zone'.

STRETCHING FOR DIFFERENT TYPES OF PHYSICAL ACTIVITY

BALLISTIC

- Rapid bouncing movements, where momentum is used to move body parts beyond their normal range of movement (RoM).

- Ballistic stretching is different to dynamic stretching, which does not involve bouncing movements.

- Advantages
  - Sport specific movements.

- Disadvantages
  - There is an increased risk of injury & a decrease in maximum strength when performed before strength training.

FLEXIBILITY

- 'To improve the range of movement (RoM) at a joint.'

STATIC

- Holding stretches in a fixed position.
- Help build flexibility.
- Aid recovery.

- Regular static stretching can maintain or increase flexibility, but some theories suggest that static stretching before exercise (especially high intensity activity) can reduce motor neurone excitability, decrease the activity of the stretch reflex, resulting in a lower force being produced by the muscles & a decrease in performance.

- Advantages
  - Most recently it has been stated that they are most beneficial post-exercise competition as part of a cool down.

- Disadvantages
  - They do not mimic sporting actions.
  - Have been found to reduce muscle capacity & explosiveness when used prior to competition.

17

PRINCIPLES OF TRAINING

SPECIFICITY

Focusses on the most appropriate way to develop the required Components of Fitness (CoF) for the sport/position.

Should be relevant to the sport/position & where possible match the activity.

Factors to consider include...

contribution of energy systems, CoF, muscle fibre types, skills & movements required in the sport/position.

FITT

- FREQUENCY
- INTENSITY
- TIME
- TYPE

Classed as above even though separate sections. Both Specificity & Progressive overload can be met by manipulating

FITT
Frequency - 'how often' performer trains.
Intensity - 'how hard'. Can be manipulated by changing length of session, increasing resistance, modify work/rest ratios. Should be specific to activity (training zones).
Time - 'how long' the length of session. Should be specific to aims & sport & can be adjusted by progressive overload.
Type - 'the method', the type of training should be specific to the aims & sport (matching), but will vary depending on the periodised training year.

OVERTRAINING

May occur when training too frequently with little/no recovery between sessions. Does not allow enough time for repair of micro tears or the replenishment of energy stores which could ultimately lead to fatigue, causing illness and/or injury.

RECOVERY

- Appropriate recovery (time) is important if continued high levels of performance are to be maintained.

- Time for recovery is dependent on the intensity of training & generally takes longer to adjust at the start of each mesocycle due to changes in intensity.

REVERSIBILITY

'Use it or lose it.' Adaptations gained through regular & progressive training will be lost if training at appropriate levels are not maintained.

This generally occurs if athletes are ill/injured for any period. For this reason, health & fitness experts are not in favour of 'total rest' & some form of optimal exercise' should be done in recovery phase.

PROGRESSIVE OVERLOAD

'More than normal', gradually working with more intensity throughout the training programme. This allows the body to adapt to incremental training demands, improving fitness levels safely & reducing the risk of injury.

Overload can be applied by... increasing duration, intensity, levels (% max HR, % 1RM, adjust work/rest ratio), more difficult exercises or increasing frequency.

PERIODISATION

There are numerous phases, including...

MACROCYCLE

- The whole training year or training cycle that can be subdivided into **3** distinct phases.

- Preparatory Phase
- Competition Phase
- Transition Phase

Focusses on the systematic variation of training to allow athletes to peak at an optimal time or times during the competition phase or season.

It divides the training year into smaller, more manageable phases.

COMPETITION PHASE (B)

The aims of this phase are to maintain fitness & conditioning & focus on 'in-season' competition skills, tactics & strategies. The volume of training decreases, but intensity increases in an attempt to mimic game/ activity intensity - clear link to specificity.

TRANSITION PHASE (C)

The main transition period is after the competition phase (off season) & athletes traditionally utilise cross-training methods here at lower intensity to maintain a level of conditioning.

During a long season or when an athlete may have to peak more than once, the competition phase may be subdivided (transition period where training is tapered between mesocycles to allow for recovery from in-season fatigue and/or injury.

MESOCYCLE

The macrocycle is broken down/ divided into various mesocycles - depending on activity & length of season. Focussed on specific areas.
e.g. power, strength.

MICROCYCLE

Each mesocycle is broken down int a weekly microcycle. Led by the aim of mesocycle, though can focus on + in performance/ training.

PREPARATORY PHASE (A)

Part 1 - General Conditioning

High volume, low intensity to develop an endurance base.
Prepares the body for further increases in intensity in future cycles.

Part 2 - Competition Specific

Training intensity gets progressively higher than in Part 1 with an increased focus on speed & strength training.
Greater focus on game techniques & tactics.

Performance peak

Intensity

Sport form

A1 A2 B C

19

FAERTLEK

- Swedish for 'speed play' & a form of continuous exercise as there are no breaks.
- Involves changes in pace/speed and or gradient/terrain.
- Also similar to interval training as periods of high & low intensity.
- Variations in intensity allow both aerobic & anaerobic energy systems to be used.
- Develops aerobic fitness/power, speed, muscular endurance.
- Intensities can be manipulated to mimic the sport/activity training for.

<u>Advantages</u> - modified to mimic game intensity, develops numerous CoF.

<u>Disadvantages</u> - difficult to track appropriate intensity level (unless monitored by coach / use wearable tech).

LEARN

- Key characteristics & +/- for each method of training listed.

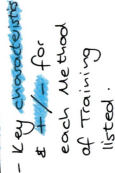

FOCUSES OF TRAINING METHODS

- **HIIT/INTERVAL** - Anaerobic Power.
- **CONTINUOUS** - Aerobic Power.
- **FAERTLEK** - Aerobic Power.
- **CIRCUIT** - Muscular Endurance.
- **WEIGHT** - Strength.
- **PNF** - Flexibility.

METHODS OF TRAINING

WEIGHTS

FREE WEIGHTS & MACHINES.

- Can be manipulated to improve muscular strength, power or muscular endurance & used to increase muscular hypertrophy.
- Recent studies show that regular strength training can decrease the risk of injury in sport.
- CoF developed is determined by the resistance, repetitions & reps performed & is usually monitored through % 1RM (85%+ = strength, 75-85% hypertrophy, strength endurance 60-70%).
- Free weight exercises are performed using dumbells, barbells and kettlebells, whereas machine weights involve the use of specialised fitness machines with weighted plates attached that work via a cam & pulley system.

<u>Advantages</u> - can be sports specific (more so with free weights), variation in single & multi-joint exercises, can focus on different CoF & adaptations (intensity dependant), can focus on specific muscle groups (more so with machines).

<u>Disadvantages</u> - may need a spotter to reduce injury risk (free weights), non-sports specific (machines), expensive (esp machines).

METHODS OF TRAINING II

to increase HR to to at least 80% of MHR, followed by short periods of lower intensity movements/rest. Advantages - burn a lot of calories in a short period, can be sports specific & can work various CoF in one session. ① Disadvantages - if intensity too high, early fatigue & overtraining.

HIGH INTENSITY INTERVAL TRAINING

- HIIT
- Is a type of interval training which incorporates several rounds that alternate between a set number of minutes of high intensity work

PROPRIOCEPTIVE NEUROMUSCULAR FACILITATION - PNF

Passive/partner assisted stretch, followed by an isometric contraction (muscle contracts but length remains same), followed by further stretching.
Advantages - increases RoM
① Disadvantages - need a partner for most stretches & can decrease muscle strength straight after stretching.

INTERVAL

- Bouts of training with rest intervals between repetitions.
- Work/rest ratio can be adapted to target both aerobic & anaerobic systems (increase work period, lower intensity).
Advantages - W:R can be adapted to target specific energy systems, times that mimic competition, increases lactate/anaerobic threshold, rest allows PC replenishment.
Disadvantages - if intensity is too high, lead to early fatigue or overtraining.

CONTINUOUS

- sustained exercise performed at low to moderate intensity (60-80% of MHR) eg run, swim, cycle.
Advantages - develops the aerobic system, minimal equipment needed, low risk of injury due to intensity levels & efficient for weight/fat loss.
Disadvantages - non sports specific (especially games), time consuming, can be boring!

CIRCUITS

- Involves a series of exercises performed at stations one after the other, with rest periods between each station.
Advantages - use simple exercises, time efficient, can do full body workout, can focus on area(s) of weakness, can be general fitness based, or sport specific or skills based. Not much equipment needed (use body weight).
① Disadvantages - can be too generic, not specialised enough, space.

FRACTURE

- **Fractures** (not a stress fracture - that is an **overuse injury**) occur **suddenly** as a result of **direct impact**, fall or a **violent twisting movement**.

- **Acute**

- These fractures are more common in collision (rugby) or contact (football) sports. They can however occur in non contact sports (such as skiing) after a fall.

The 2 main types of fractures are...

INCLUDES

- **DISLOCATIONS**
- **FRACTURES**
- **STRAINS**
- **SPRAINS**

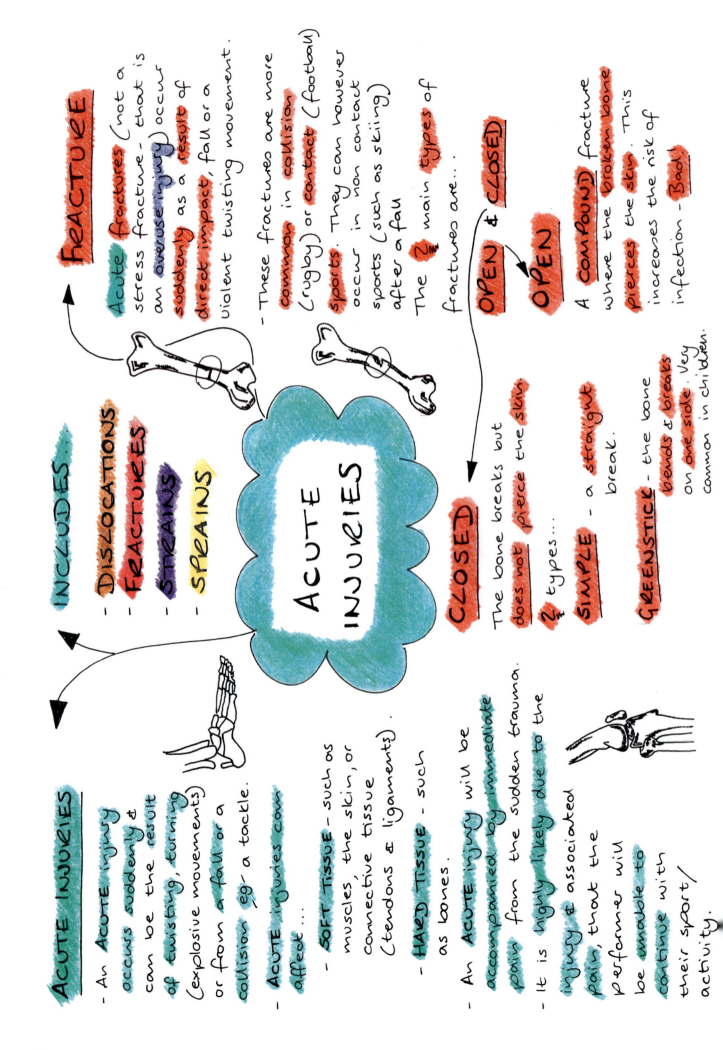

ACUTE INJURIES

OPEN & CLOSED

OPEN

A **COMPOUND** fracture where the broken bone pierces the skin. This increases the risk of infection - Bad.

CLOSED

The bone breaks but does not pierce the skin. 2 types...

SIMPLE - a straight break.

GREENSTICK - the bone bends & breaks on one side. Very common in children.

ACUTE INJURIES

- An **ACUTE** injury occurs suddenly & can be the result of twisting, turning (explosive movements) or from a fall or a collision eg - a tackle.

- **ACUTE** injuries can affect ...

  - **SOFT TISSUE** - such as muscles, the skin, or connective tissue (tendons & ligaments).

  - **HARD TISSUE** - such as bones.

- An **ACUTE** injury will be accompanied by immediate pain from the sudden trauma.

- It is highly likely due to the injury & associated pain, that the performer will be unable to continue with their sport/activity.

ACUTE INJURIES II

STRAIN

- Torn muscle or tendon.
- 'A tear,' or the 'pulling of a muscle.'
- An acute injury, though without proper preparation & rehabilitation, chronic pain & re-occurrence can occur.
- Strains tend to occur in muscles that cross 2 joints, such as the quadricep group, hamstring group, groin and gastrocnemius.
- Regardless of severity, proper rehabilitation is required to ensure full recovery & to limit the chance of re-occurrence.

DISLOCATION

- Occurs due to trauma dislodging the bone from a joint.
- This type of injury is more likely to occur & performers are more susceptible when the muscles & tendons that surround a joint are weak, or if there is an imbalance.
- Common sites for dislocation include fingers, shoulder & knee
- frequently occurs in rugby & cricket from the impact of the ball, or rugby from a tackle or collapsed scrum.

SPRAIN

- 'A tear of a ligament.'
- Therefore decreases the stability & support of a joint.
- There are 3 common areas where sprains occurs.

ANKLE - inversion/eversion twisting.

KNEE - sudden twist damages collateral ligaments.

WRIST - falling on an outstretched hand.

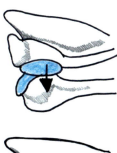

PCL   ACL

CHRONIC INJURIES

STRESS FRACTURES

- Are a micro-fracture caused by too much stress on a bone & trauma that gradually develops over time.
- Additional risk factors include...
- Repetitive high impact exercise
- High training frequency & intensity
- Not adhering to appropriate application of the principles of training.
  - Poor nutrition
  - Improper technique
  - Improper clothing/technique.
- Most common stress fractures include...
- Metatarsal bones in the foot (long distance runner)
- Vertebrae (fast bowlers - cricket).

Overuse

Overuse injuries are more subtle & occur over time, making them more difficult to diagnose & treat. Generally caused by repetitive micro-trauma to soft tissue, joints & bones as a result of poor technique, over training surfaces, equipment, over training or returning too soon after injury.

TENDONITIS

- Repetitive loading of a tendon, exceeding ability to handle load
- Caused by...
- High training frequency & intensity
- Biomechanical errors in technique
- Training surfaces
- Inappropriate equipment
- Muscle imbalance
- Inadequate recovery time.

Common tendonitis injuries occur in the knee, achilles & elbow.

GOLFERS ELBOW

Or medial epicondylitis causes pain & inflammation on medial part of elbow (inside). Not just in golf, racquet sports also where clench fist & repeatedly use wrists.

TENNIS ELBOW (outside)

Or lateral epicondylitis causes pain & inflammation of the tendon that attaches on the lateral part of the elbow. Not just common in tennis, swinging racquet/bat sports eg cricket.

ACHILLES TENDONITIS

- This is an overuse injury of the Achilles tendon, the band of tissue that connects the gastrocnemius muscle at the back of the lower leg to the heel bone.
- Achilles tendonitis most often occurs in runners, where they have suddenly increased the duration or intensity of the runs.
- To help recover from achilles tendonitis, it is important to rest and immobilise the affected area.
- Ice & heat therapy can also help reduce pain & inflammation
- Progressive stretching & strengthening exercises to prevent further injury & promote healing is important.

PREVENTION OF INJURIES

MUSCLE BALANCE

- Muscle imbalance results from weakness, poor flexibility and/or low/poor endurance.
- Common injuries caused by muscle imbalances include...
- Hamstring muscle tightness/weakness can put strain on the ACL, quadriceps & cause knee pain.
- Rotator cuff injuries can also be caused by over-tight pectoral muscles.
- A balanced strength programme is required to minimise injury.

PROTECTIVE EQUIPMENT

- Protective equipment in elite sport is generally enforced by most teams, clubs, NGB's & sponsors, to ensure injuries are minimised.
- eg helmets for batting in cricket, helmets for cycling, mouthguards in hockey, rugby & boxing, correct gloves in boxing.

MANAGING RISKS

- NGB's conduct a review of rules in order to prevent injury. eg law adjustment to scrums in rugby.

SCREENING

- Is used to assess the level of risk that exercise &/or performance could potentially have on a performer's health.
- Can be conducted through a combination of methods, such as a PARQ (Physical Activity Readiness Questionnaire), a fitness test battery, CRY (Cardiac Risk in the Young) test through an ECG (Electrocardiogram) to test the health of the heart.
- Screening can at times be unreliable and cause anxiety.
- However, most professional sports teams undertake a (full) medical & require a health report prior to a transfer/trade/swap deal taking place.

TECHNIQUE

- Practising/training with repetitive poor technique can lead to injuries such as stress fractures & tendonitis.
- Using biomechanical analysis apps & a qualified coach can help to alleviate any issues with technique to minimise injuries & maximise performance.

25

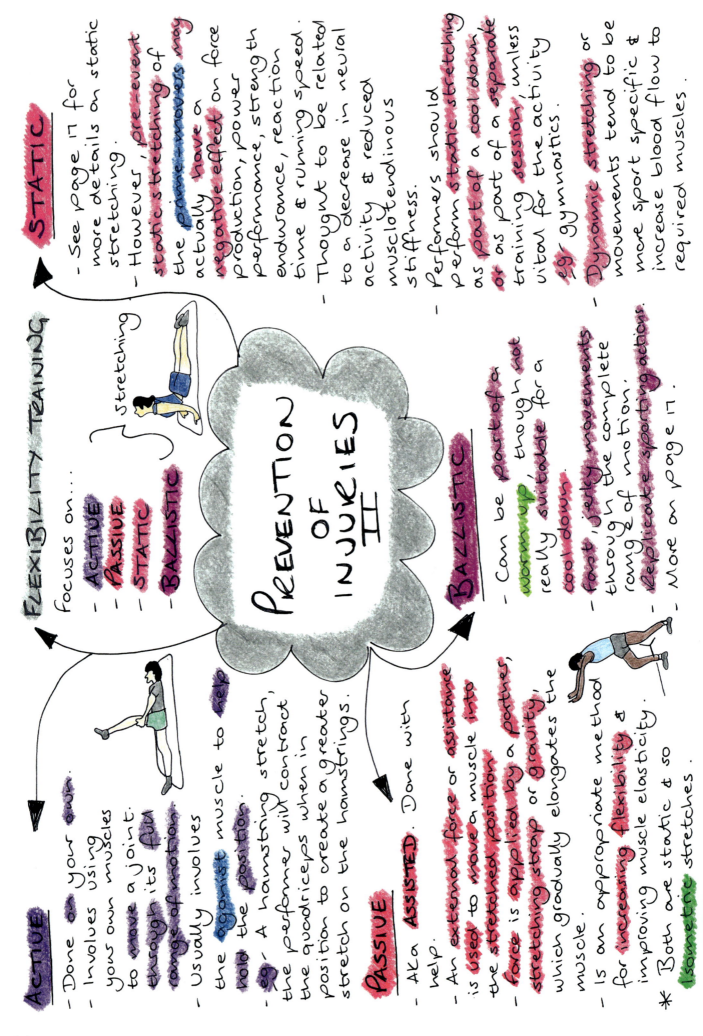

FLEXIBILITY TRAINING

Focuses on...
- ACTIVE
- PASSIVE
- STATIC
- BALLISTIC

} stretching

PREVENTION OF INJURIES II

ACTIVE

- Done on your own.
- Involves using your own muscles to move a joint through its full range of motion.
- Usually involves the agonist muscle to help hold the position.
- eg. A hamstring stretch, the performer will contract the quadriceps when in position to create a greater stretch on the hamstrings.

PASSIVE

- Aka ASSISTED. Done with help.
- An external force or assistance is used to move a muscle into the stretched position.
- Force is applied by a partner, stretching strap or gravity, which gradually elongates the muscle.
- Is an appropriate method for increasing flexibility & improving muscle elasticity.
* Both are static & so isometric stretches.

STATIC

- See page 17 for more details on static stretching.
- However, prevent static stretching of the same movers may actually have a negative effect on force production, power performance, strength endurance, reaction time & running speed.
- Thought to be related to a decrease in neural activity & reduced musclotendinous stiffness.
- Performers should perform static stretching as part of a cool down or as part of a separate training session, unless vital for the activity eg. gymnastics.
- Dynamic stretching or movements tend to be more sport specific & increase blood flow to required muscles.

BALLISTIC

- Can be part of a warm up, though not really suitable for a cool down.
- Fast, jerky movements through the complete range of motion.
- Replicate sporting actions.
- More on page 17.

26

PREVENTION OF INJURIES III

USE OF A WARM UP
- A thorough, full 4 stage (if appropriate) warm up should be completed
- This should be done prior to any physical activity.
- gradual pulse raiser
- stretching
* skill based practices
* mental preparation if appropriate
- More on page 16.

NEOPRENE
- In sport, this is generally used to support a part of the body.
- It is a 'rubbery' synthetic material that retains heat & so can help reduce swelling.
- Commonly found in knee braces & shoulder supports.

BANDAGING
- May be used to immobilise a sprained joint.
- Limits movement & reduces blood flow.
- May also be used on cuts & lacerations to stem blood flow & to cover the wound.

TAPING & BRACING
- Provide support to the performer.

KINESIOLOGY TAPING
- May relieve pain by improving the stability of a joint.
- Kinesiology tape is really stretchy!
- It mimics the elasticity of the skin & allows the performer to use their full range of motion.
- When applied, it slightly shrinks, lifting the skin, creating a tiny space between skin & tissue (muscles, tendons).
- This increases space & aids blood flow.
- It also improves circulation & reduces swelling

INJURY REHABILITATION METHODS

PROPRIOCEPTIVE TRAINING

- Used to develop strength, mobility & flexibility.
- Can be used after injury.
- Stretch muscle (with partner) to upper limit & hold
- Repeat stretch. ⇒ further.
- Inhibits stretch reflex

STATIC PASSIVE

- More on page 21.

HYPERBARIC CHAMBERS

Hyperbaric therapy is a treatment where 100% O_2 is administered under pressure greater than the atmospheric O_2 pressure.

The process pressurises the blood vessels within the body for 60-120 mins, to accelerate the recovery of soft tissue micro-tears, hence decreasing the risk/effect of DOMS.

The idea is to recover more quickly, exercise for longer to help maximise performance levels.

HYDROTHERAPY

Cold water therapy has been proven to reduce muscle soreness & increase/improve recovery times. In addition, contrast water therapy for a duration of 14-15 mins has been shown to improve performance.

STRENGTH TRAINING

- Applying a structured periodis yearly plan & the application of appropriate (principles of training (progressive overload) will ensure a performers body is ready for the demands of their sport.

- More injuries occur in the latter stages of a game, therefore conditioning is crucial.

- A study published in "British Journal of Sports Medicine in 2018 stated there was a significant reduction of acute injuries as a result of strength training. This could be a result of increased strength & size of muscles & adjacent tissue, a decrease in critical joint loads & improved coordination, as well as having psychological benefits. eg increased confidence.

CRYOTHERAPY

Each session can last between 2-4 mins & involves exposing the body to extremely low temperatures generated by liquid nitrogen. The theory behind this method, explains that vasoconstriction of blood vessels occur, reducing blood flow. Once treatment finishes, vessels then dilate, flushing waste products from the body, assisting the lymphatic system & improving recovery.

RECOVERY FROM EXERCISE

COLD THERAPY

- Helps reduce swelling (oedema) & tissue breakdown.
- Vasoconstriction occurs, reducing blood flow to assist in reducing swelling, as well as slowing down metabolic activity & nerve impulses (which may explain why it aids in reducing pain also).

Normal   Vasodilation   Vasoconstriction

- Ice water immersion has also shown to be able to shift lactate.

CRYOTHERAPY

- see previous page.

PHYSIOLOGICAL REASONS FOR METHODS USED

HYPERBARIC CHAMBERS & CRYOTHERAPY -
see previous page.

ICE BATHS

Believed to decrease/reduce inflammation & increase recovery rates. Blood vessels constrict & then dilate when you get out. This process helps to flush out metabolic waste at the end of an intense training session or Performance.

MASSAGE

This is widely used as a recovery strategy to reduce muscle soreness & to stimulate blood flow. However, most evidence does not support massage as an effective method to improve/increase recovery of functional performance.

It is thought that massage is more beneficial for prevention & management of injury, as well as providing a psychological boost to the performer.

FOAM ROLLERS

- A form of self massage. Different levels of 'hardness' can be purchased to meet individual needs.
- After an intense bout of exercise, foam rolling is thought to alleviate muscle fatigue, DOMs & improve muscular performance.
- Can help prevent myofascial adhesions ('knots or trigger points) from forming as new muscle is built.
- Some S&C coaches recommend foam rolling after any workout & also the day after (if heavy).

COMPRESSION GARMENTS

- Increases blood flow to muscles & increases venous return to disperse waste products.
- Better used post exercise for recovery rather than during. Thought to reduce intramuscular space available for swelling, thereby decreasing DOMs.

29

THE IMPORTANCE OF SLEEP & NUTRITION FOR IMPROVED RECOVERY

SLEEP

- There are 2 main stages of sleep ...

1 - REM (Rapid Eye Movement). Sleep is a time of significant brain activity & is believed to be essential for cognitive functions.

- eg. memory, learning & creativity.
- Dreams occur in this stage.

2 - Non REM, or NREM is the phase of sleep where your body physically recovers/repairs itself from the day.

HOW DOES SLEEP AID MUSCLE RECOVERY?

- Muscle growth and repair. The body releases Human Growth Hormone (HGH) during sleep which stimulates protein synthesis to help repair muscle fibre microtears.

- Muscle glycogen replenishment. Especially with at least 8 hrs of sleep to replenish both liver & muscle glycogen stores after intense exercise & to ensure that muscles have enough fuel for optimal performance.

* Not enough sleep = the opposite!

- Hormonal regulation. Sleep helps regulate testosterone levels. This is released during sleep & promotes muscle growth & repair.

- Inflammation reduction. Intense exercise can cause muscle damage & inflammation. During sleep the body produces anti-inflammatory cytokines.

- Muscle relaxation: sleep helps release tension & promote recovery.

POST PERFORMANCE NUTRITION

Importantly there are 2 windows

1st Window - consume high GI CHO foods within the first 30 mins to enhance post exercise refuelling of muscle glycogen.

- Maintain hydration & electrolyte balance. This allows blood plasma levels to gradually return to normal, the reducing blood viscosity & increases transport of vital nutrients for recovery

2nd Window - consume CHO within the first 2 hrs to increase recovery rate. This speeds up the replenishment of glycogen stores.

- Protein should also be included to help speed up the recovery from micro tears. This is particularly important for high intensity/strength & power based performers.

3.2.1 Exercise physiology

1. **Describe** a sports-related function for the following nutrients:

   a. Calcium   (2 marks)

   b. Protein   (2 marks)

   c. Vitamin D   (2 marks)

2. **Explain** how an endurance athlete can manipulate their diet in preparation for an event.   (6 marks)

3. **Analyse** the benefits of taking supplements in preparation and for recovery from physical activity.   (8 marks)

4. **State** a negative effect of taking the following supplements:

   a. Caffeine   (1 mark)

   b. Sodium bicarbonate   (1 mark)

   c. Creatine Monohydrate   (1 mark)

5. **Describe** the difference between quantitative and qualitative data.
                                                       (2 marks)

6. **Explain** the difference between validity and reliability with regards to fitness testing.   (4 marks)

7. **Identify** the physiological benefits of a warm-up to the performer.
                                                       (4 marks)

8. **Assess** whether a warm-up reduces the chances of injury in sport.
                                                       (8 marks)

9. **Examine** when static and ballistic stretching would benefit an athlete.

(6 marks)

10. With reference to the listed principles of training below:

- Specificity

- Progressive overload

- Reversibility

a **Define** each principle. (3 marks)

b **Describe** how the principles of training can be applied successfully in a training programme. (3 marks)

11. **Explain** the purpose of the preparation, competition and transition phases of a periodised training programme. (6 marks)

12. **Describe** the difference between a macro, meso and microcycle with regards to periodisation of training. (3 marks)

13. **Describe** an advantage and disadvantage of circuit training for a netball player. (2 marks)

14. **Explain** when PNF stretching would be benefit for an athlete.

(4marks)

15. **Describe**, using examples, the difference between an acute injury and a chronic injury. (4 marks)

16. **Identify** (a) and **classify** (b) the descriptions of injuries below:

i) Swelling and inflammation of a tendon   (2 marks)

ii) Fatigue-induced small crack in a weight-bearing bone.   (2 marks)

iii) A force that pulls or stretches a muscle or tendon.   (2 marks)

iv) Separation of articulating bones.   (2 marks)

v) Stretching or tearing of ligaments that causes swelling. (2 marks)

17. **Explain** four ways in which sports performers can try and prevent injuries.

(8 marks)

18. **Discuss** the use of hyperbaric chambers v cryotherapy in the recovery from injuries.

(8 marks)

Total marks   /81

3.2.2: Biomechanical movement

3.2.2.1: Biomechanical principles

What students need to learn		Yes	Nearly	No
Newton's Three Laws of linear motion applied to sporting movements.	First law (inertia), second law (acceleration), third law (action/reaction). Force.			
Definitions, equations and units of example scalars.	Speed, distance.			
Centre of mass.				
Factors affecting stability.	Height of centre of mass, area of base of support, position of line of gravity and body mass.			

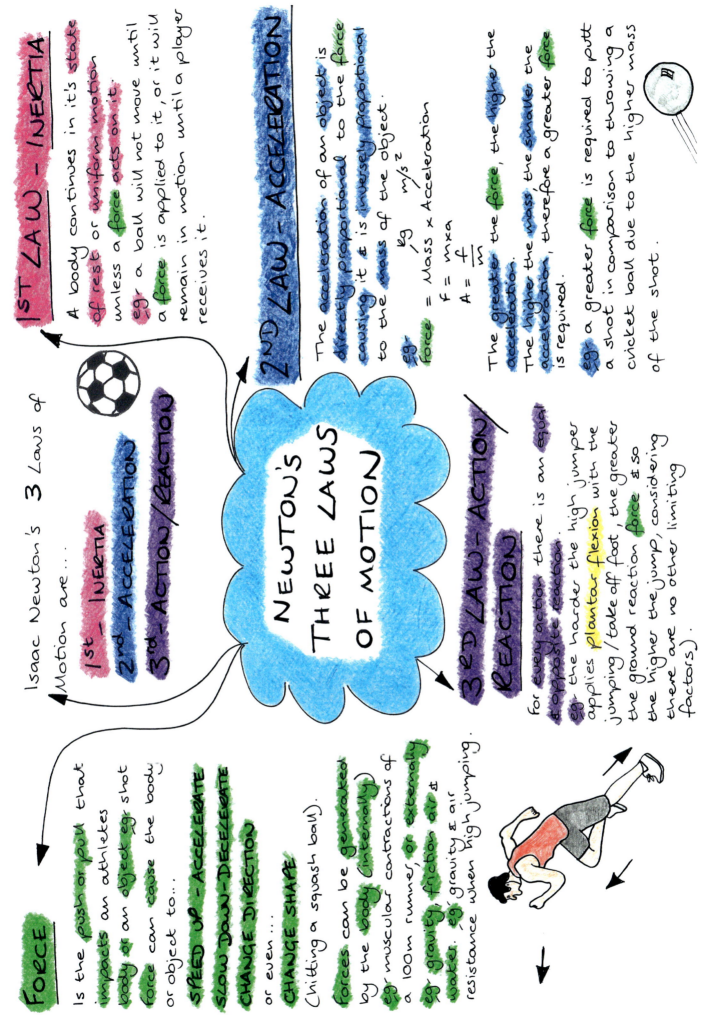

1ST LAW – INERTIA

A body continues in it's state of rest or uniform motion unless a force acts on it.
eg a ball will not move until a force is applied to it, or it will remain in motion until a player receives it.

Isaac Newton's 3 Laws of Motion are...

1st – INERTIA
2nd – ACCELERATION
3rd – ACTION/REACTION

NEWTON'S THREE LAWS OF MOTION

2ND LAW – ACCELERATION

The acceleration of an object is directly proportional to the force causing it & is inversely proportional to the mass of the object.

eg m/s^2

Force = Mass × Acceleration

$$F = m \times a$$
$$A = \frac{f}{m}$$

The greater the force, the higher the acceleration.
The higher the mass, the smaller the acceleration, therefore a greater force is required.

eg a greater force is required to putt a shot in comparison to throwing a cricket ball due to the higher mass of the shot.

3RD LAW – ACTION/REACTION

For every action there is an equal & opposite reaction.

eg the harder the high jumper applies plantar flexion with the jumping/take off foot, the greater the ground reaction force & so the higher the jump, (considering there are no other limiting factors).

FORCE

Is the push or pull that impacts an athletes body or an object eg shot force can cause the body or object to...

SPEED UP – ACCELERATE
SLOW DOWN – DECELERATE
CHANGE DIRECTION

or even...

CHANGE SHAPE
(hitting a squash ball).

forces can be generated by the body (internally) eg muscular contractions of a 100m runner, or externally eg gravity, friction air & water. eg gravity & air resistance when high jumping.

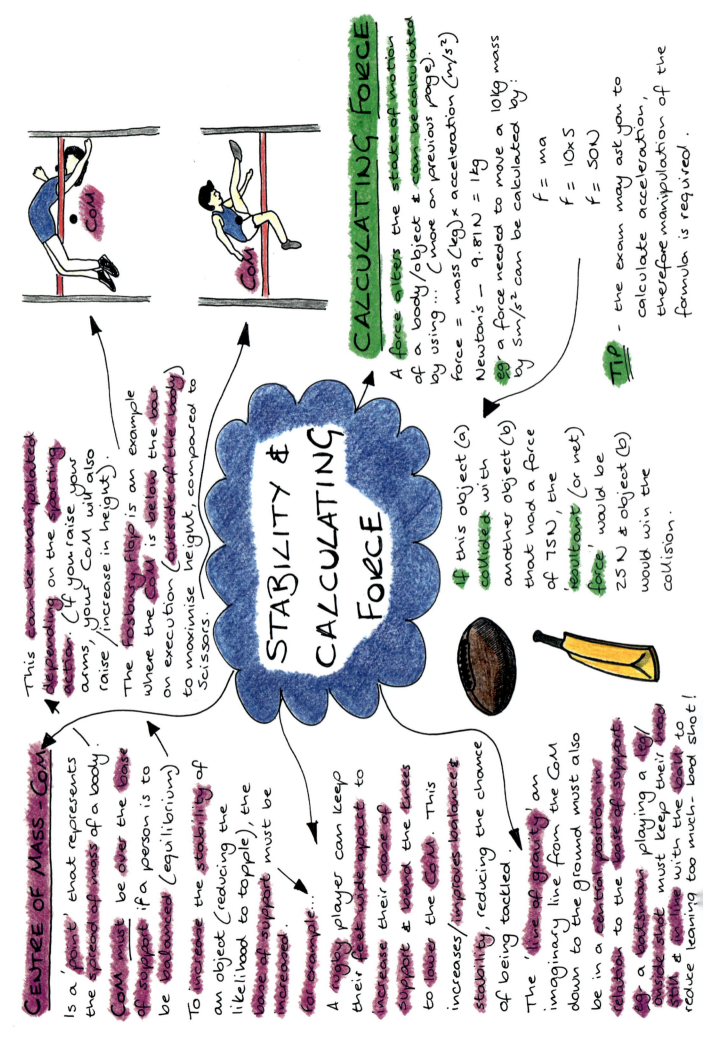

CENTRE OF MASS - CoM

Is a 'point' that represents the spread of mass of a body.

CoM must be over the base of support if a person is to be balanced (equilibrium)

To increase the stability of an object (reducing the likelihood to topple), the base of support must be increased.

for example...

A rugby player can keep their feet wide apart to increase their base of support & bend their knees to lower the CoM. This increases/improves balance & stability, reducing the chance of being tackled.

The 'line of gravity' an imaginary line from the CoM down to the ground must also be in a central position in relation to the base of support.

eg a batsman playing a leg/ onside shot must keep their head still & online with the ball to reduce leaning too much- bad shot!

This can be manipulated depending on the sporting action. (If you raise your arms, your CoM will also raise/increase in height).

The Fosbury flop is an example where the CoM is below the bar on execution (outside of the body) to maximise height, compared to scissors.

STABILITY & CALCULATING FORCE

CALCULATING FORCE

A force alters the state of motion of a body/object & can be calculated by using... (more on previous page).

force = mass (kg) × acceleration (m/s²)

Newton's — 9.81N = 1kg

eg a force needed to move a 10kg mass by 5m/s² can be calculated by :

$$F = ma$$
$$F = 10 \times 5$$
$$F = 50N$$

TIP - the exam may ask you to calculate acceleration, therefore manipulation of the formula is required.

If this object (a) collided with another object (b) that had a force of 75N, the 'resultant' (or net) 'force' would be 25 N & object (b) would win the collision.

3.2.2.2: Levers

What students need to learn	Yes	Nearly	No
Three classes of lever and examples of their use in the body during physical activity and sport.			
Mechanical advantage and mechanical disadvantage of each class of lever.			

MECHANICAL ADVANTAGE & DISADVANTAGE

Key Terms

EFFORT ARM - the distance between the effort & fulcrum. The greater the comparison to the resistance arm, the greater the mechanical advantage. (1st & 2nd class levers). However, 3rd class levers have a mechanical disadvantage due to the small effort arm (though allows for quick movements over a large range).

RESISTANCE (LOAD) ARM - the distance between the load, resistance & fulcrum. Both 1st & 2nd class levers create a mechanical advantage as the fulcrum is closer to the load (shorter resistance arm) & a larger effort arm, though 2nd class levers have a higher mechanical advantage. A heavier load can therefore be lifted with less effort.

$$\frac{Effort\ Arm}{Resistance\ Arm} = Mechanical\ Advantage\ (MA)$$

LEVERS

Levers in the body are made up of bones, ligaments, tendons & muscles that enable human movement.

A lever consists of...

FULCRUM - the pivot around which the lever moves (a joint).

LOAD - what you are trying to move (resistance)

EFFORT - the force applied to + **LEVER** arm (bone). move the load.

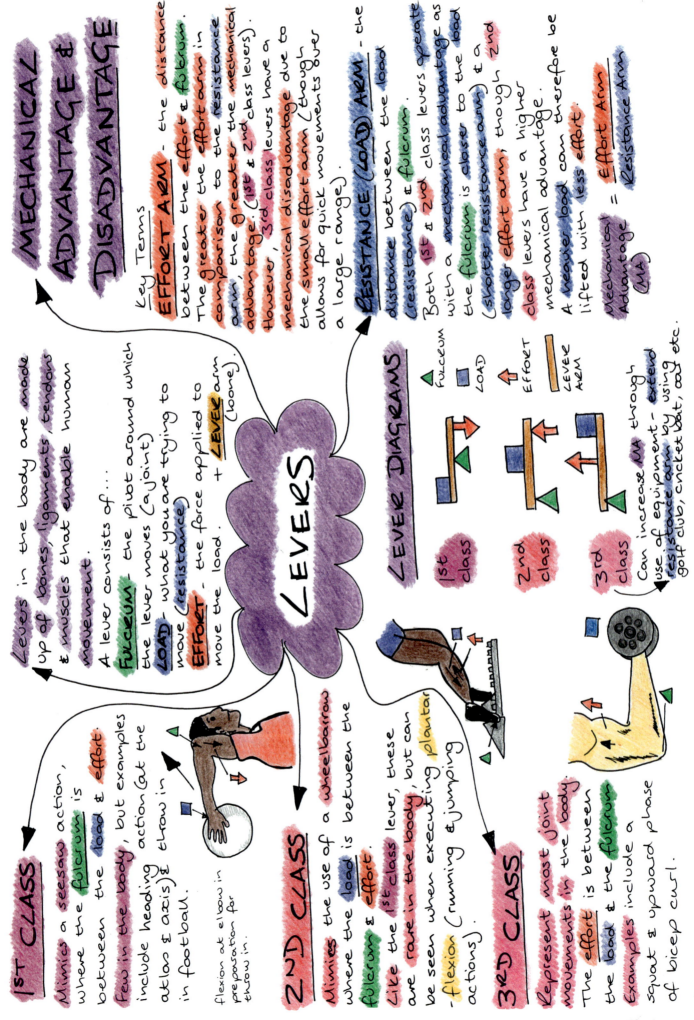

LEVER DIAGRAMS

△ FULCRUM
▣ LOAD
⬆ EFFORT
▬ LEVER ARM

1st class
2nd class
3rd class

Can increase MA through use of equipment - extend resistance arm by using golf club, cricket bat, oar etc.

1st CLASS

Mimics a seesaw action, where the fulcrum is between the load & effort.

Few in the body, but examples include heading action (at the atlas & axis) & throw in in football.

Flexion at elbow in preparation for throw in.

2nd CLASS

Mimics the use of a wheelbarrow where the load is between the fulcrum & effort.

Like the 1st class lever, these are rare in the body, but can be seen when executing plantar-flexion (running & jumping actions).

3rd CLASS

Represent most joint movements in the body.

The effort is between the load & the fulcrum.

Examples include a squat & upward phase of bicep curl.

3.2.2.3: Linear motion

What students need to learn		Yes	Nearly	No
An understanding of the forces acting on a performer during linear motion.	Gravity, frictional force, air resistance, internal-muscular force, weight.			
Definitions, equations and units of vectors.	Weight, velocity, displacement, acceleration and momentum.			
Definitions, equations and units of scalars.	Mass, speed and distance.			
The relationship between impulse and increasing and decreasing momentum in sprinting through the interpretation of force/time graphs.				

FORCES ACTING ON A PERFORMER DURING LINEAR MOTION

FRICTIONAL FORCES

- Friction acts AGAINST the movement of one surface over another. eg. trainers on the road when running.

- friction is the force that PREVENTS a performer from slipping & acts in the OPPOSITE direction to the force the foot applies on the track/road & in the SAME direction as the movement.

- If one or more of the surfaces are ROUGH, this will INCREASE the amount of friction.

- There are though sporting activities performed on ALMOST FRICTIONLESS surfaces.

- for example, in ice skating, the blades GLIDE OVER the ice, generating heat, which in turn causes the ice to melt.

The ice LOOSENS & the water acts as a lubricant which creates a smooth surface for the ice skate to perform their routine on.

GRAVITY

- The force of gravity acts on objects in a direction that is PERPENDICULAR to level ground.

- for example, if an object is moving PARALLEL to the ground ie a chest pass in netball, the force of gravity is only pulling on the object in a DOWNWARD direction.

- The force is NOT affected by SIDEWAYS motion & simply pulls the object down at the same rate as if it was stationary.

Moving Ball.

40

FORCES ACTING ON A PERFORMER DURING LINEAR MOTION II

- Since the formula for force =

$$force = mass \times acceleration$$

the greater the force produced by a performer, the **GREATER** the change in velocity/**acceleration**

- e.g. the larger/greater the force of the muscle contraction of the quadriceps & gastrocnemius when sprinting, the **FASTER** the sprinter travels.

WEIGHT

- Sometimes weight & mass are used **INTERCHANGEABLY**.
- Mass is a measure of how much matter there is in an object, or how dense it is.
- Weight is a measure of the size of the pull of gravity on an object.
- The **MOTION** of a body on the horizontal plane is affected with more weight as more **FORCE** is required to move it.
- e.g. more force is required in the muscle contractions of a sprinter who weighs more than another sprinter.

INTRA-MUSCULAR FORCE

- In order to move an object, a **FORCE** must be applied to it.
- A force can also be applied **INTERNALLY** via muscle contractions.

AIR RESISTANCE

- Is a frictional force that **SLOWS** an object's forward motion.
- The amount of air resistance on an object/body depends on the following...

- The **VELOCITY** the object is travelling at. The greater the velocity, the greater the air resistance.

- The size of the **CROSS SECTIONAL** area of the object. Increased size means increased air resistance.

- The **SHAPE** of the object. A more streamlined shape helps allow the object to move through the air more easily.

- The **SURFACE** of the object. A smoother surface means there is less turbulence & so it moves through the air with less resistance.

- Advances in technology & technique adjustment has allowed cyclists to reduce air resistance by **CROUCHING** LOW on their bikes to make them go faster. They also have more streamlined equipment so that air passes over them more easily, reducing the effect air resistance has on their performance.

41

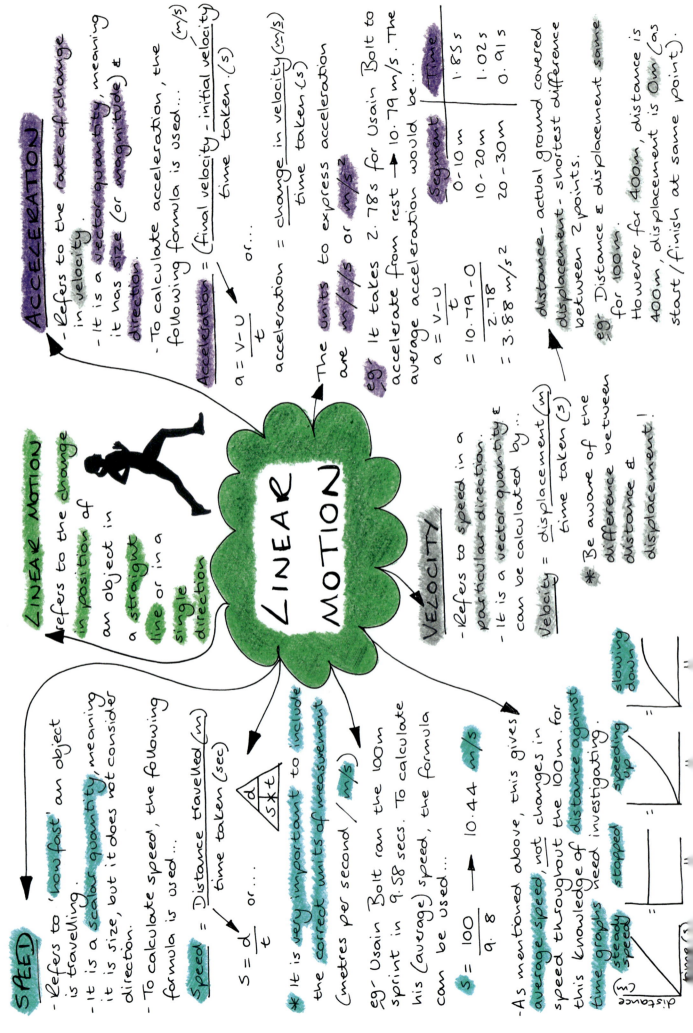

LINEAR MOTION

ACCELERATION

- Refers to the rate of change in velocity.
- It is a vector quantity, meaning it has size (or magnitude) & direction.
- To calculate acceleration, the following formula is used... (m/s)

$$\text{Acceleration} = \frac{(\text{final velocity} - \text{initial velocity})}{\text{time taken (s)}}$$

$$a = \frac{v-u}{t}$$

or...

$$\text{acceleration} = \frac{\text{change in velocity (m/s)}}{\text{time taken (s)}}$$

The units to express acceleration are m/s/s or m/s²

e.g. It takes 2.78s for Usain Bolt to accelerate from rest to 10.79 m/s. The average acceleration would be...

$$a = \frac{v-u}{t}$$
$$= \frac{10.79-0}{2.78}$$
$$= 3.88 \text{ m/s}^2$$

Segment	Time
0-10m	1.85 s
10-20m	1.02 s
20-30m	0.91 s

distance - actual ground covered
displacement - shortest difference between 2 points.

e.g. Distance & displacement same for 100m. However for 400m, distance is 400m, displacement is 0m (as start/finish at same point).

LINEAR MOTION

refers to the change in position of an object in a straight line or in a single direction

SPEED

- Refers to 'how fast' an object is travelling.
- It is a scalar quantity, meaning it is size, but it does not consider direction.
- To calculate speed, the following formula is used...

$$\text{Speed} = \frac{\text{Distance travelled (m)}}{\text{time taken (sec)}}$$

$$s = \frac{d}{t}$$

or...

[triangle: d / s x t]

* It is very important to include the correct units of measurement (metres per second / m/s)

e.g. Usain Bolt ran the 100m sprint in 9.58 secs. To calculate his (average) speed, the formula can be used...

$$s = \frac{100}{9.8} \rightarrow 10.44 \text{ m/s}$$

- As mentioned above, this gives average speed, not changes in speed throughout the 100m. For this knowledge of distance against time graphs need investigating.

slowing down
speeding up
stopped
steady speed

distance / time (s)

VELOCITY

- Refers to speed in a particular direction.
- It is a vector quantity & can be calculated by...

$$\text{Velocity} = \frac{\text{displacement (m)}}{\text{time taken (s)}}$$

* Be aware of the difference between distance & displacement.

MASS

- As has been explained previously, mass is a measure of **HOW MUCH** matter there is in an object.

- **INERTIA** (resistance to acceleration) is a property of **mass**, meaning the higher the **mass**, the greater the **inertia**.

- **FORCE** is...

- Therefore more force is required to move an object with a **LARGER mass** compared to an object with a **LIGHTER mass** in order to maintain the **SAME acceleration**

- Using the formula $F = m \times a$ helps explain this concept.

- for example, a 100m sprinter who is 100 kg will have to produce **MORE** force to **accelerate** at the same level as a sprinter who is 90 kg.

* **VELOCITY**
  SPEED,
  ACCELERATION &
  DISTANCE - See P42

DISTANCE - See P42

DEFINITIONS, EQUATIONS & UNITS OF VECTORS & SCALARS

WEIGHT

- is 9.81N (Newtons) for each kg of **MASS**, though this is sometimes rounded to 10 N/kg.

- eg. if a sprinter has a **mass** of 75 kg, their weight would be $75 \times 10 = 750$ N (or $75 \times 9.81 = 735.75$N)

MOMENTUM (P)

MASS (m) × **VELOCITY** (V) =

$85 kg \times 7.5 m/s = 637.5 kg/m/s$

$100 kg \times 7.5 m/s = 750 kg/m/s$

LINEAR MOMENTUM

- Refers to the **PRODUCT** of **mass** × velocity.

- the **MOMENTUM** = **mass** × velocity.

- It is a **VECTOR** as it has **MAGNITUDE** & **DIRECTION**.

- If an athlete can achieve the same **VELOCITY** with a higher **MASS**, they will be **STRONGER** than before & create more **MOMENTUM**.

- eg. If a rugby player was 85 kg last season & can run with a velocity of 7.5 m/s, his **momentum** would be 637.5 kg/m/s.

- However, if the same rugby player adds **BULK** for the next season (up to 100 kg) & can still run with the **SAME velocity**, his **momentum** would now be 750 kg/m/s, making it harder to complete a tackle in a game.

IMPULSE & INCREASING & DECREASING MOMENTUM

INCREASING & DECREASING MOMENTUM IN SPRINTING

- At the start of the race, the heel strike produces a negative impulse.

- However, with the drive phase on take off, a positive impulse is produced. Result = acceleration. Overall - net positive impulse.

force+ (N)

Time (s)

- With constant landing/take off actions of the foot, there are both positive & negative impulses during the middle of the race. Equal each other out = running at constant velocity.

force+ (N)

0 Time (s)

- At the end of the race, the net impulse is negative & the sprinter is decelerating, as more frequent heel strikes on the ground rather than force produced on take-off.

+ force (N)

0 Time (s)

- An impulse can be calculated as follows...

IMPULSE = FORCE × TIME (Newton seconds)

- More information on UNITS can be seen on page 42.

IMPULSE

- An impulse is the time it takes for a force to be applied to an object.

- An object's change in MOMENTUM is EQUAL to its IMPULSE.

- It is the INCREASE or DECREASE in an object's momentum.

- An INCREASE in impulse will mean there is an INCREASE in the rate of change of momentum, leading to a change in VELOCITY.

- eg- a footballer will follow through in their shot at goal in the execution phase, all the way through to the recovery, in order to MAXIMISE foot to ball contact.

- The INCREASE in momentum leads to the ball travelling FASTER.

- IMPULSE can also be used to DECREASE momentum.

- eg- when a javelin thrower releases the javelin, they will have to STOP quickly to stop themselves from going over the foul line/falling. They do this by increasing contact time of foot/ground to quickly DECELERATE.

3.2.2.4: Angular motion

What students need to learn		Yes	Nearly	No
Application of Newton's laws to angular motion.				
Definitions and units for angular motion.	Angular displacement, angular velocity, angular acceleration.			
Conservation of angular momentum during flight, moment of inertia and its relationship with angular velocity.				

ANGULAR MOTION

MOMENT OF INERTIA

- Inertia is the 'amount of force required to move a mass in a straight line.'

- Moment of inertia (or rotational inertia) uses the same concept, but relates to rotational movement.

- Therefore, the further away a mass is from the axis of rotation the more 'spread out' the mass is. This would increase the moment of inertia & more force would be needed to move it/slow it down.

eg. a gymnast performing a somersault in an open position (arms & legs extended) will have a large moment of inertia as the mass of the body will spread away from the axis of rotation, & therefore will spin slowly.

ANGULAR MOTION

- ANGULAR MOTION is defined as... 'the motion of a body/mass about a fixed point or axis.' (rotating or spinning action). The same principles used for LINEAR MOTION in terms of velocity, displacement & acceleration apply to angular motion.

As the gymnast looks to land, the limbs will move out & away from the axis of rotation increasing MI & decreasing angular velocity in order to slow the spin/rotations so they can land safely.

ANGULAR MOMENTUM

- Refers to the product of angular velocity & moment of inertia.

ANGULAR MOMENTUM = MI × ANGULAR VELOCITY

Therefore if MI increases, angular velocity decreases & vice versa, providing there is no other force acting on the object. eg air resistance. If there are no outside forces acting on the rotating object/body, then angular momentum is conserved (as there is no change in total angular momentum).

eg a gymnast performing a somersault will tuck their body in to decrease MI & increase angular velocity. ie increase rate of spin/rotations.

NEWTON'S LAWS

- **NEWTON'S** laws are usually associated with **LINEAR MOTION**.

- However, they are relatable to **ANGULAR MOTION** also.

- Angular motion occurs as a result of **MOMENT** **FORCE** or **TORQUE**.

- Torque causes an object to rotate about an **axis**, therefore it is known as a **TURNING** or **ROTATIONAL FORCE**.

REMEMBER

- Isaac Newton's 3 laws of motion are...

- 1st law - **INERTIA**
- 2nd law - **ACCELERATION**
- 3rd law - **ACTION / REACTION**.

APPLICATION OF NEWTON'S LAWS TO ANGULAR MOTION

1st LAW - INERTIA

- A body in rotation will continue its rotation with a constant **angular velocity** unless acted on by an external **torque**.

- eg - a diver will continue to rotate while being 'tucked in', doing a somersault until the diver starts to spread their limbs in preparation for the dive entry into the water.

- This increases the **moment of inertia**, leading to a decrease in **angular velocity**.

2nd LAW - ACCELERATION

- **Angular acceleration** of an object is directly proport-ional to the net **torque** acting on it & inversely proportional to its mass rotational inertia.

- eg - when a golf ball is struck by a golf club, the rate of change of momentum of the ball

- (or velocity) is proportional to the size of the force/torque acting on it by the club.

- More **torque** means faster rotation.

APPLICATION OF NEWTON'S LAWS PLUS DEFINITIONS AND UNITS FOR ANGULAR MOTION

ANGULAR ACCELERATION

- Angular acceleration represents the rate of change in angular velocity & is a vector quantity.

- When velocity is increasing, the acceleration is in the same direction of rotation (to increase the velocity).

- When the velocity is decreasing, there has to be an acceleration in the opposite direction of travel, acting as a brake to decrease the velocity.

- eg. angular acceleration increases for a gymnast spinning anti-clockwise.

DEFINITIONS

ANGULAR DISPLACEMENT

- The angle in radians through which a point or line has been rotated in a specific sense about a specified axis.

- It is the angle of the movement of a body in a circular path.

ANGULAR VELOCITY

UNITS

Angular velocity = Angle turned (radians) / Time taken (s)

Angular Acceleration = Change in Angular velocity (radians/s) / Time taken to change (s)

3rd LAW - ACTION/REACTION

- For every torque, there is an equal and opposite reaction torque.

- eg. when a cheerleader is standing on the ground (at rest), her momentum is 0 (zero), because she is not moving.

- In order for her to complete a backflip, she could jump up at a slight angle (providing initial angular momentum) & then tuck her limbs in.

- Initial torque is created when pushing off the ground with an equal & opposite reaction torque.

3.2.2.5: Projectile motion

What students need to learn		Yes	Nearly	No
Factors affecting horizontal displacement of projectiles.				
Factors affecting flight paths of different projectiles.	Shot putt, badminton shuttle.			
Vector components of parabolic flight.				

TRANSLATIONAL MOVEMENT

- When the **POSITION** of the object has **changed**.
- eg- when a squash ball is hit, it moves forward towards the back wall of the court.

ROTATIONAL MOVEMENT

- When the force applied causes the ball to **ROTATE**.
- eg- playing a backhand slice in tennis or squash.

PROJECTILE MOTION

- Projectile motion refers to either...
  - An object. eg- a javelin
  - The human body.
  - eg- long/high jump as the body travels/flies through the air.

PROJECTILE MOTION

FORCES

- Act on the flight of a projectile.
- Include...
  Gravity
  Air Resistance
  Lift forces (more on page 54.).

FORCE

- Produces **3** types of movement.

DEFORMATIVE MOVEMENT

- When the **SHAPE** of an object changes.
- eg- when a squash ball is hit, it changes shape or 'squashes' the ball.

Ball stretches in falling

As the ball falls, it's speed increases

Ball at highest slows

resumes natural shape

As balls hits, it is squashed.

VECTORS

- Have **MAGNITUDE** (size) & **DIRECTION** and represent the different components illustrated in both the **PARABOLIC** (shot putt) & **NON-PARABOLIC** (shuttlecock) diagrams by arrows.
- The size of the arrow indicates the size of the magnitude. ie the **BIGGER** the arrow, the **GREATER** the magnitude.

PROJECTILE MOTION II

GRAVITY

- If GRAVITY was not present, a projectile would travel in a constant straight line.

- HOWEVER, gravity (9.81 ms⁻²) causes a projectile to travel in a PARABOLIC TRAJECTORY (see below)

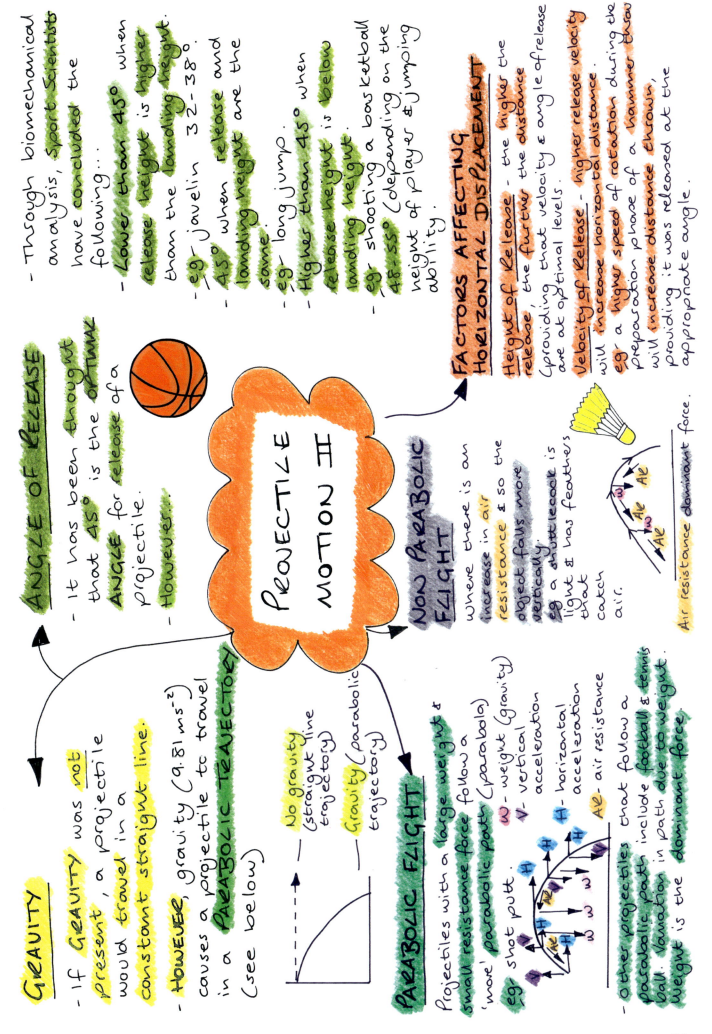

— No gravity (straight line trajectory)

— Gravity (parabolic trajectory)

ANGLE OF RELEASE

- It has been thought that 45° is the OPTIMAL ANGLE for release of a projectile.

- However...

- Through biomechanical analysis, Sport Scientists have concluded the following...

- Lower than 45° when release height is higher than the landing height.
 - eg. Javelin 32-38°.

- 45° when release and landing height are the same.
 - eg. long jump.

- Higher than 45° when release height is below landing height.
 - eg. shooting a basketball 48-55° (depending on the height of player & jumping ability.

FACTORS AFFECTING HORIZONTAL DISPLACEMENT

Height of Release - the higher the release, the further the distance (providing that velocity & angle of release are at optimal levels.

Velocity of Release - higher release velocity will increase horizontal distance.
eg. a higher speed of rotation during the preparation phase of a hammer throw will increase distance thrown, providing it was released at the appropriate angle.

PARABOLIC FLIGHT

Projectiles with a large weight & small resistance force follow a 'more' parabolic path (parabola)

- eg. shot putt.

W - weight (gravity)
V - vertical acceleration
H - horizontal acceleration
AR - air resistance

- Other projectiles that follow a parabolic path include football & tennis ball. Variation in path due to weight. Weight is the dominant force.

NON PARABOLIC FLIGHT

where there is an increase in air resistance & so the object falls more vertically.
eg. a shuttlecock is light & has feathers that catch air.

Air resistance dominant force.

51

3.2.2.6: Fluid mechanics

What students need to learn		Yes	Nearly	No
Dynamic fluid force.	Drag and lift.			
Factors that reduce and increase drag and their application to sporting situations.				
The Bernoulli principle applied to sporting situations.	Upward lift force (discus). Downward lift force (speed skiers, cyclists, racing cars).			

FLUID MECHANICS

HYDRODYNAMICS

- Refers to the flow of water around a projectile which can influence the speed & direction of travel.
- Ways in which swimmers can reduce drag
  - streamline body position & flat in water.
  - lean bodies
  - minimise turbulent flow by...
- wear tight fitting swimsuits
- swimming hats
- remove hair
- maximise 15m distance underwater at the start & on turns to reduce drag from turbulence on the surface. (Dolphin kick).

The Speedo LZR Racer swimsuit is now banned, why?
- 'technical' doping
- compressed the swimmers body into a stream lined 'tube'.
- trapped air 'inside suit', adding buoyancy to the swimmer & ultimately reducing the level/amount of drag.

Fluid mechanics considers objects that move through the AIR (Aerodynamics) or WATER (Hydrodynamics). It involves the forces acting against moving objects within these mediums & how they slow them down.

AERODYNAMICS

- Refers to the flow of air around a projectile which can influence the speed & direction of travel. (Aerodynamic drag or drag force).
- Air resistance can be affected by several factors, including...
- Velocity - an increase in velocity leads to increased air resistance opposing the object.
- Shape - the more aerodynamic the object, the lower the resistance.
- Cross-Sectional area (Frontal) - the smaller the frontal cross-sectional area, the lower the air resistance. eg. crouching down low when cycling downhill.
- Smoothness of surface - the smoother the surface, the lower the air resistance. (See below)

Direction of travel →

The wake is an low pressure zone. It is larger for a rough surface ball, therefore more drag.

Smooth   rough   Air flow   wake

Goes further

This is the same concept with cycling helmets. The more stream lined (decreased frontal cross sectional area) - leads to a decreased low pressure zone to reduce drag & increase speed

Direction of travel

However, with a golf ball, the dimples have been designed to create an attach-detach-attach again system that creates tiny pockets of turbulence so that the air flow is close to the ball, decreasing the wake & decreasing the low pressure zone.

'Less wake & so less drag - low pressure zone minimised'

turbulence

LIFT FORCES

BERNOULLI EFFECT

- As the velocity of a fluid increases, the pressure exerted by the fluid decreases.
- Since forces will always act from an area of high pressure to an area of low pressure, an uplift is created, providing high pressure is below the projectile.
- e.g. In discus - more lift is needed during flight to maximise the distance thrown. In this case, the angle of attack will be important as the discus will need to be tilted at the most appropriate angle.

Direction of throw

Lift ↑

Drag

air has longer to travel, so
velocity ↑
pressure ↓

angle of attack

air flow at
velocity ↓ & so
pressure ↑

- Pressure moves from a high to low & as a result, a lift force is created. & the discus stays in the air for longer.
- If the angle of attack is too high, drag increases, therefore reducing the lift.
- The optimum angle of release for a discus is approximately 35°, however the angle of attack is between 26 - 38°

DOWNWARD LIFT FORCE

- The Bernoulli principle does not just explain upward lift force. It can also be used to explain the benefits of downward force.
- This benefits activities such as speed skiers, cyclists and racing cars.

SPEED SKIERS

- Need to maintain good contact with snow/ice.
- This helps to heat the snow/ice leading to a 'more' frictionless surface that increases velocity.

RACING CARS

- Similar to cycling, a downward lift force on a racing car is accelerated by its aerodynamic features.
- The features include the wings (which create downforce) and the diffuser (which increases the amount of airflow under the car). The shape of the Formula 1 car's body is also important, affecting how air moves around the car.
- Downforce increases vertical force on the tyres, increasing grip & thus allowing the car to travel faster.

CYCLISTS

- Cyclists crouch down to form a more stream-lined position over the handlebars, meaning that air travelling over the cyclist has a shorter distance to travel.
- The air travels at a slower velocity, leading to a higher pressure creating a downward lift force meaning the tyres have more grip on the road/track.

54

3.2.2: Biomechanical Movement

1. At the start of a 100m sprint, the runner must push off the starting blocks as quickly as possible to get a good start.

a. Using Newton's First Law of Motion, **explain** how the sprinter pushes off the starting blocks. (2 marks)

b. Using Newton's 2nd Law of Motion, **explain** how the sprinter pushes off the starting blocks. (2 marks)

c. **Calculate** the force needed to allow the sprinter to accelerate if he/she has a mass of 85kg and at 3.75m/s/s. (2 marks)

d. Using Newton's Third Law of Motion, **explain** how the sprinter pushes off the starting blocks. (2 marks)

2. **Identify** two ways in which a rugby player can maintain balance in a contact situation. (2 marks)

3. If two footballers collide during a tackle, with player A having a resultant force of 144N and player B 168N, calculate the following:

a. Resultant force: (1 mark)

b. If player B was accelerating at 3m/s/s, what was his/her mass (kg). Show working. (2 marks)

4. **Draw** diagrams of each lever system, labelling the key elements. (3 marks)

5. Using a sporting example, **explain** why a 2nd class. lever has a mechanical advantage.

(4 marks)

6. The table below shows the breakdown of Usain Bolt's 100m sprint performance in the 2008 Beijing Olympics. The table outlines the split times and cumulative times for every 10m.

Splits (10m)	10m Split times (s)	Cumulative time (s)	Average speed (m/s)
0–10	1.85	1.85	
10–20	1.02	2.87	
20–30	0.91	3.78	
30–40	0.87	4.65	
40–50	0.85	5.50	
50–60	0.82	6.32	
60–70	0.82	7.14	
70–80	0.83	7.96	
80–90	0.83	8.79	
90–100	0.90	9.69	
Total Time	9.69	9.69	

a. **Calculate** the average speed for every 10m and the overall average speed for the 100m (write your answer in the table above) (10 marks)

b. **Calculate** Usain Bolt's acceleration between:

i)   0-25m   (2 marks)

ii)   25-50m   (2 marks)

iii)   50-75m   (2 marks)

iv)   75-100m   (2 marks)

v)   **Give** reasons for differences in acceleration rates between the two parameters mentioned in i) and ii).   (3 marks)

c. Using the grid below, complete the following:

i)   **Plot** the results from the table in the distance against time graph below.   (1 mark)

ii)   **Shade** the area of the graph where the sprinter accelerated the most.   (1 mark)

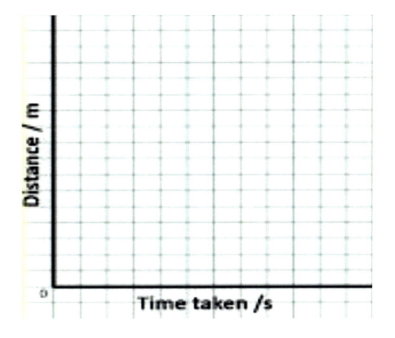

6. The following graphs show displacement against time.

Each graph is labelled A to E:

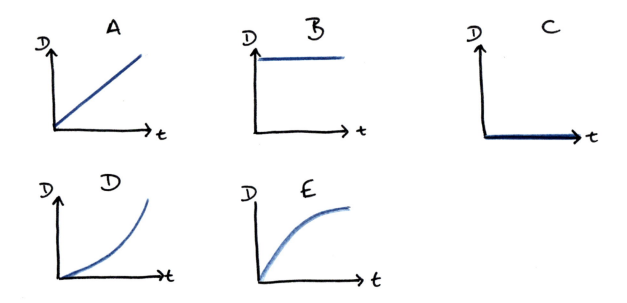

Which graph is displaying the following?

    i)   Acceleration   (1 mark)

    ii)   0 velocity and 0 displacement   (1 mark)

    iii)   Constant speed   (1 mark)

    iv)   0 velocity   (1 mark)

    v)   Deceleration   (1 mark)

7. The figure below shows an ice skater:

a. **Identify** what makes up a performer's 'moment of inertia?'

(2 marks)

b. Using the figure above, **explain** how the ice skater can adjust their rate of spin.

(4 marks)

8. **Identify** the factors that affect horizontal displacement.

(3 marks)

9. The flight paths of different objects can be parabolic or non-parabolic.

a. **Define** parabolic.

(1 mark)

b. **Describe** the main factors that limit the distance that a golf ball will travel in flight.

(3 marks)

c. **Compare** the flight of a golf ball with a shuttlecock.

(4 marks)

10. **Explain** how the angle of release is different with various projectile based sporting activities.

(6 marks)

11. **Identify** three factors that affect fluid friction and air resistance.

(3 marks)

12. **State** strategies a swimmer could do to lessen the effect of fluid friction whilst swimming.

(3 marks)

13. The discus is also an athletic event where maximising horizontal displacement is key to winning the event.

Analyse how the **Bernoulli effect** will affect the flight path and the displacement of the discus.

(8 marks)

14. In table tennis it is possible to apply spin on the ball when playing various shots.

Examine how the player, using his/her knowledge of the **Magnus effect** can apply this? (8 marks)

Total marks /93

3.2.3 Sport Psychology

What students need to learn			Yes	Nearly	No
3.2.3.1.1: Aspects of personality	Understanding of the nature vs nurture debate in the development of personality.	Trait, social learning.			
	Interactionist perspective.	Hollander, Lewin.			
	How knowledge of interactionist perspective can improve performance.				
3.2.3.1.2: Attitudes	Triadic model.	Components of an attitude. Formation of attitudes. Changing attitudes through cognitive dissonance and persuasive communication.			
3.2.3.1.3: Arousal	Theories of arousal.	Drive theory, inverted U theory, catastrophe theory and zone of optimal functioning theory.			
	Practical applications of theories of arousal and their impact on performance.				
	Characteristics of peak flow experience.				

3.2.3.1.4: Anxiety	Types of anxiety.	Somatic, cognitive, competitive trait and competitive state.			
	Advantages and disadvantages of using observations, questionnaires and physiological measures to measure anxiety.				
3.2.3.1.5: Aggression	Difference between aggression and assertive behaviour.				
	Theories of aggression.	Instinct theory, frustration-aggression hypothesis, social learning theory and aggressive cue theory.			
	Strategies to control aggression.				
3.2.3.1.6: Motivation	Motivation.	Intrinsic, extrinsic, tangible and intangible.			
3.2.3.1.7: Achievement motivation theory	Atkinson's Model of achievement motivation.				
	Characteristics of personality components of achievement motivation.	Need to achieve (Nach) and Need to avoid failure (Naf).			
	Impact of situational component of achievement motivation.	Incentive value and probability of success.			
	Achievement goal theory.	Impact of outcome orientated goals and task orientated goals.			

	Strategies to develop approach behaviours leading to improvements in performance.				
3.2.3.1.8: Social facilitation	Social facilitation and inhibition.	Zajonc's model.			
	Evaluation apprehension.				
	Strategies to eliminate the adverse effects of social facilitation and social inhibition.				
3.2.3.1.9: Group dynamics	Group formation.	Tuckman's model			
	Cohesion.	Task and social.			
	Steiner's model of potential and actual productivity, faulty group processes.	Including cooperation and coordination.			
	Ringelmann effect and social loafing.				
	Strategies to improve cohesion, group productivity and overcome social loafing to enhance team performance.				
3.2.3.1.10: Importance of goal setting	Benefits of types of goal setting.	Outcome goals, performance related goals, process goals.			
	Principles of effective goal setting.	SMARTER (specific, measurable, achievable, realistic, time bound, evaluate, re-do).			
3.2.3.1.11: Attribution theory	Attribution process.				
	Weiner's Model and its application to sporting situations.				
	Link between attribution, task persistence and motivation.				
	Self-serving bias.				

	Attribution retraining.				
	Learned helplessness.	General and specific.			
64	Strategies to avoid learned helplessness leading to improvements in performance.				
3.2.3.1.12: Self-efficacy and confidence	Characteristics of self-efficacy, self-confidence and self-esteem.				
	Bandura's Model of self-efficacy.	Performance accomplishments, vicarious experiences, verbal persuasion and emotional arousal.			
	Vealey's Model of self-confidence.	Relationship between trait sport confidence, competitive orientation, the sport situation and state sport confidence.			
	Effects of home field advantage.				
	Strategies to develop high levels of self-efficacy leading to improvements in performance.				
3.2.3.1.13: Leadership	Characteristics of effective leaders.				
	Styles of leadership.	Autocratic, democratic, laissez-faire.			
	Leadership styles for different sporting situations.				
	Prescribed and emergent leaders.				

	Theories of leadership in different sporting situations.	Fiedler's contingency theory and Chelladurai's multi-dimensional model.			
3.2.3.1.14: Stress management	Explanation of the terms 'stress' and 'stressor'.				
	Use of warm up for stress management.				
	Effects of cognitive and somatic techniques on the performer.				
	Explanation of cognitive techniques.	Mental rehearsal. Visualisation. Imagery. Attentional control and cue utilisation. Thought stopping. Positive self-talk.			
	Explanation of somatic techniques.	Biofeedback, centering, breathing control, progressive muscle relaxation.			

65

TRAIT THEORY

- Trait theories see personality as being innate (born with) & that it is stable & predictable in all situations.

- It is heredity & passed on through genes.

- This means that behaviour is easier to predict in all situations, with the environment & the situation not playing much part in affecting personality.

- eg· a players personality will not change if it is a regular season game or play-off final.

- The drawback to the trait theory of personality is that the environment & learning situations are not taken into account & that behaviour is not always predictable.

PERSONALITY THEORIES

HOLLANDER (1971)

defined personality as a 'combination of all the characteristics that make a person unique.'

PERSONALITY

... refers to individual differences in characteristic patterns of ...

- thinking
- feeling
- behaving.

- No 2 people have exactly the same type of personality.

- People behave in different ways in relation to various circumstances, reflecting an individual's most prominent characteristics, highlighting greater importance of personality traits in sport.

FOCUS ON ...

- EYSENCK (1975)
- CATTELL (1957)
- HOLLANDER (1971)
- LEWIN

EYSENCK

EXTROVERTS
- Crave excitement & take risks.
- Become bored easily.
- Tend to perform better with higher arousal levels
- Extroverts prefer activities that involve gross motor skills, so team games are more favourable.
- Continuous/endurance activities (eg marathon running) are less appealing.

INTROVERTS
- Quiet & reserved
- Already 'over aroused', so do not seek extra stimulation.
- Introverts prefer to take part in activities that require more precision (eg archery). Fine motor skills.

UNSTABLE
- or NEUROTIC personality traits are changeable, varied & so behaviour is unpredictable.
- eg a performer's mood can swing from situation to situation & suffer from higher levels of stress.

STABLE
- Are unchangeable, consistent & so behaviour is predictable.
- eg if a tennis player generally possesses less anxiety in a particular situation, they will then possess lower levels of anxiety in all situations.

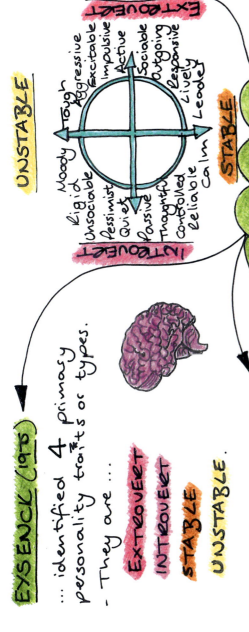

EYSENCK (1975)
- ...identified 4 primary personality traits or types.
- They are ...
  - EXTROVERT
  - INTROVERT
  - STABLE
  - UNSTABLE.

- One way of explaining the extrovert/introvert continuum is based on Eysenck's work.

He argues that the difference between extroverts & introverts is because extroverts inherit an 'underaroused' nervous system & therefore seek extra stimulation.

- More specifically, part of the brain called the Reticular Activating System (RAS) can determine whether an athlete is more inclined to be an extrovert or an introvert.

UNSTABLE
EXTROVERT
- Tough
- Moody
- Aggressive
- Excitable
- Impulsive
- Active
- Sociable
- Outgoing
- Responsive
- Lively
- Leader

- Rigid
- Unsociable
- Pessimist
- Quiet
- Passive
- Thoughtful
- Controlled
- Reliable
- Calm
INTROVERT

STABLE

SOCIAL LEARNING THEORY

- states that individuals develop their personality through environmental factors rather than traits we are born with.

- Learning from significant others & role models, parents & peers.

- People especially children model their behaviour by watching others (live more impactful than media).

- According to BANDURA, there are 4 stages of modelling.

ATTENTION - usually paying attention to someone respected & wanting to imitate.

RETAIN - remember the actions & response displayed.

REPRODUCTION - try the behaviour; aim to receive the same response as their role model (strengthens behaviour).

MOTIVATION - If the individual receives the response they were looking for, they will be more likely to reproduce the behaviour.

Attention Retain Reproduction Motivation

CATTELL

The SOURCE TRAITS are the 16 factors

The SURFACE TRAITS are the low score & high score columns.

These are the traits on the continuum.

SOURCE TRAITS

- The most important & found at the top of the continuum.

SURFACE TRAITS

- Influence behaviours at different intensities & regularity.

CATTELL'S TRAIT THEORY (1957)

- According to Cattell, there is a hierarchy of personality traits.

- From previous studies he was able to apply factor analysis to reduce [7] characteristics to 16 key personality factors.

- Cattell believed that there was a continuum of personality traits & that each person contained all of these 16 traits, to a certain & variable degree. ie high in some people but low in others.

- These personality traits were either ...

SOURCE TRAITS

or

SURFACE TRAITS

HOLLANDER'S (1971) PERSONALITY STRUCTURE

- States the structure has 3 layers

PSYCHOLOGICAL CORE

- Basic attitudes & values that remain relatively constant.
- Influences responses.

TYPICAL RESPONSE

- the way someone responds to any given situation.
- based on the performers attitudes & beliefs (psychological core).
- eg. cricketer 'walking' when out as reflects good etiquette & sportsmanship / fairplay.

ROLE - RELATED BEHAVIOUR

- Behaviour is influenced by the situation or environment.
- May be totally different / have no resemblance to the psychological core (depending on strength of the pressures in the environment.
- eg. a player may have to adjust to suit their new role i.e team leader / captain.

Role Related Behaviour

Typical Response

Psychological Core

INTERACTIONIST PERSPECTIVE

- A coach could recognise certain situations in a game can make certain performers more anxious. eg. taking free throws in basketball.
- Here, the coach can use certain stress-inhibiting strategies, support & encouragement to assist the performer.
- Training sessions to focus on areas of weakness / struggles could be mimicked in with suggested strategies to overcome.
- Understand what actions trigger individuals - sub them off.

IMPROVE PERFORMANCE

- A coach can use their knowledge of the interactionist perspective to help the team or individual. How?

INTERACTIONIST

- This perspective suggests that we behave as a result of our innate core personality (genetic traits) & as a result of the environment (social learning).

- Interactionists see

BEHAVIOUR (B) as being a FUNCTION (f) of both a PERSONALITY (P) & the ENVIRONMENT (e).

- This therefore equates to ...

$$B = f(P \cdot e)$$

or

$$B = f(P \times e)$$

This explains how a rugby player may be quite shy & reserved off the pitch, but their behaviour changes to assertive & confrontational on it.

COGNITIVE

- Knowledge & information help form a belief. eg you believe that doing **weight training** will develop muscle tone, keep you strong & enhance body image.

AFFECTIVE

- The emotional response to an 'attitude object'. eg you enjoy the training regime & completing with training partners.

BEHAVIOURAL

- Behaviours towards an 'attitude object'. eg you complete weight training 3 times per week.

COGNITIVE - knowledge & beliefs

AFFECTIVE - feelings & emotions

BEHAVIOURAL - intended behaviour

WOOD'S MODEL

- Has **3** elements
  - COGNITIVE
  - AFFECTIVE
  - BEHAVIOURAL

WOOD'S TRIADIC MODEL

COGNITIVE

ATTITUDE

BEHAVIOURAL

AFFECTIVE

TRIANDIS (1971)

- Defines attitude as... 'ideas charged with emotion (positive and negative) which predisposes a class of actions to a particular social situation.'

- Attitudes are directed towards people, places or a situation & can be called 'attitude objects'.

- Factors that form attitudes are learnt from past experiences, family, peers & the environment, including...

  - teachers
  - coaches
  - feedback
  - media
  - culture

... rather than being **innate** (born with).

ATTITUDES AND BEHAVIOUR

PREJUDICE

- 'An extreme or strongly held attitude that is resistant to change, held previous to a direct experience.'

- If an attitude is based on false information & it is unfair, then this becomes a PREJUDICE (extreme attitude towards a person/situation).

PREJUDICE = to 'pre-judge'.

- Pre-judging a person can lead to a certain expectancy of behaviour leading to

STEREOTYPING (general inclination to place a person in categories according to an easy & identifiable set of characteristics).

- Is rarely accurate but very resistant to change.

- egs include...

- Boys are more competitive than girls.

- Black people are not very good at swimming.

- White people are not very good at 'explosive' sports
...White Men Can't Jump!

METHODS OF ATTITUDE CHANGE

- Sports professionals (managers, coaches), need to change a performer's negative attitude to a positive one.

- Helps to focus & increase the likelihood of more consistent performances.

- Some attitudes are harder to change due to STEREOTYPES & wider social issues.

PERSUASIVE COMMUNICATION

- Persuasion through communication (verbal &/or physical) is effective if delivered by a 'significant other' (influential person respected).

- The effectiveness depends on...

- If the 'persuader' is respected t a significant other.

- Appropriateness & quality of the message (makes sence, accurate & clear).

- The characteristics of the person being persuaded. Able to accept & understand the message

STRATEGIES (to change performers attitudes).

- Use positive role models to demonstrate positive attitudes.

- Give positive reinforcement of correct behaviour/attitudes.

- Agree targets/goals with the performer.

- Reward successful elements of performance.

- Give performers appropriate roles & responsibilities.

FESTINGER - COGNITIVE DISSONANCE THEORY (1957)

- States that all 3 elements involved with attitude (Triadic model - previous page) should be consistent if the attitude is to remain stable & create a feeling of CONSONANCE (positive attitude).

- If elements conflict (2 or more), this causes DISSONANCE (dishармony). Leads to the person feeling uncomfortable & so attitudes are more likely to change due to the person wanting to become more comfortable, with 1 belief dominant.

DRIVE THEORY

- Devised by **HULL (1943)** & then subsequently reviewed by **SPENCE & SPENCE (1968)**

- **Drive Theory** is ... 'a proportional linear relationship between **arousal & performance**, ie. as **arousal increases, performance increases** in proportion to arousal.

- However, this is dependent on the learned **DOMINANT RESPONSE**.

- For an elite athlete or a performer at the **autonomous stage of learning**, the **DOMINANT RESPONSE** tends to be correctly learnt & they are able to deal (appropriately with higher levels of arousal).

- For a **novice** performer (beginner) in the **cognitive stage of learning**, the **DOMINANT RESPONSE** tends to be an incorrect action & there would be a decrease in performance. This would reflect a **negative** linear relationship between **arousal & performance**

- It is important to monitor the application of pressurised scenarios for **novice** performers as this may lead to a **decrease in motivation** - **DRIVE REDUCTION**

When looking at **AROUSAL**, various **factors** must be considered, including...

- situational factors
- stages of learning
- personality.
- task differences

AROUSAL

As well as **HULL'S DRIVE THEORY**, the **INVERTED U HYPOTHESIS** & the **CATASTROPHE THEORY** must be covered (see pages 74-75).

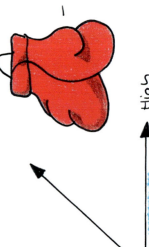

High

High ← Performance

Low ← Arousal → High

WEINBERG & GOULD (2007)

- Define arousal as ... 'a blend of physiological & psychological activity in a person and it refers to the level of motivation, alertness and excitement at a particular moment.

- Arousal can also be defined (in short) as, 'the level of psychological readiness.'

EFFECTS OF AROUSAL

- The sports performer can be both **OVER & UNDER** aroused.

- Both of these can lead to a **DECREASE** in performance.

- This will affect a performer's **concentration & motivation** levels, both of which are closely linked to arousal levels.

INVERTED U HYPOTHESIS

INVERTED U

- Devised by **YERKES & DODSON** (1908), they state that the Inverted U theory/hypothesis... 'considers that optimal performance occurs when the performer reaches an optimal level of arousal.'

- As **arousal** increases, so too does **performance**, until an optimal level, or **zone** has been reached.

- Any further increases in **arousal** will cause a decrease in **performance**.

- Certain **sports/activities** require higher/lower arousal levels for optimum performance.

- In explosive/collision type sports, such as rugby & boxing, performers often 'psych themselves up' or get 'pumped up' due to the nature of the sport.

- On the other hand, activities such as archery & shooting require calmness & concentration & so optimal levels of arousal will be lower.

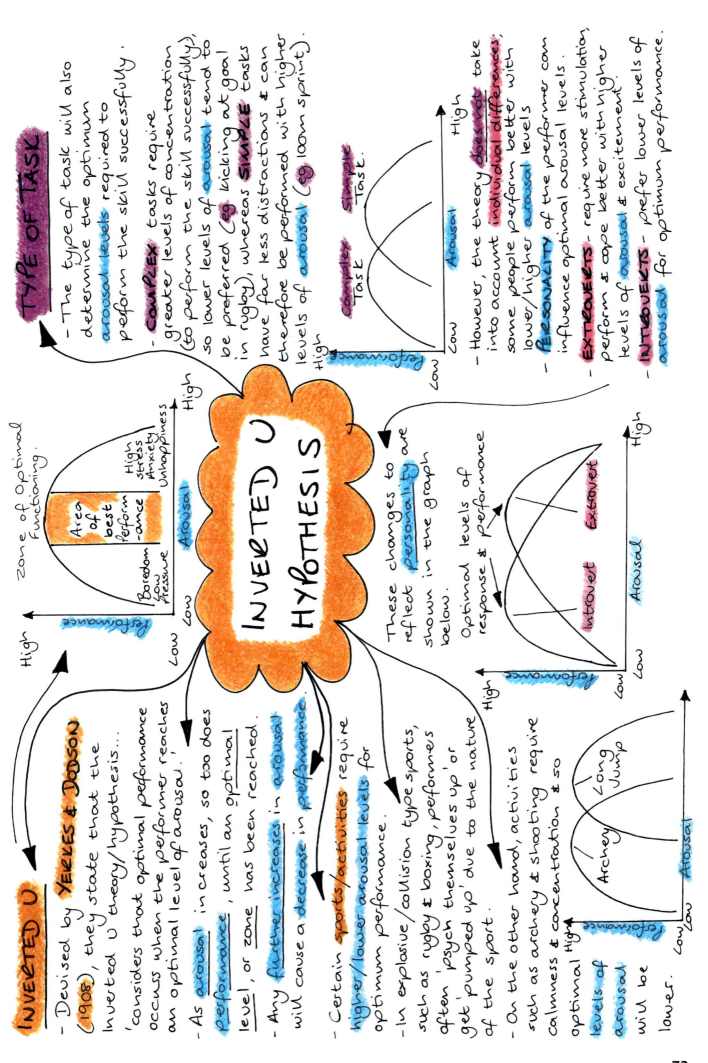

(graph: Performance (Low–High) vs Arousal (Low–High) — Long Jump, Archery)

(graph: Performance (Low–High) vs Arousal (Low–High) — Zone of Optimal Functioning. Boredom, Low Pressure; Area of best perform-ance; High stress, Anxiety, Unhappiness)

TYPE OF TASK

- The type of task will also determine the optimum **arousal levels** required to perform the skill successfully.

- **COMPLEX** tasks require greater levels of concentration (to perform the skill successfully), so lower levels of **arousal** tend to be preferred (eg kicking at goal in rugby), whereas **SIMPLE** tasks have far less distractions & can therefore be performed with higher levels of **arousal** (eg 100m sprint).

(graph: Performance (Low–High) vs Arousal (Low–High) — Simple Task, Complex Task)

- However, the theory does not take into account **individual differences**, some people perform better with lower/higher **arousal** levels.

- **PERSONALITY** of the performer can influence optimal arousal levels.

- **EXTROVERTS** - require more stimulation, perform & cope better with higher levels of **arousal** & excitement.

- **INTROVERTS** - prefer lower levels of **arousal** for optimum performance.

These changes to reflect **personality** are shown in the graph below.

(graph: Performance (Low–High) vs Arousal (Low–High) — Optimal levels of response & performance; Introvert, Extrovert)

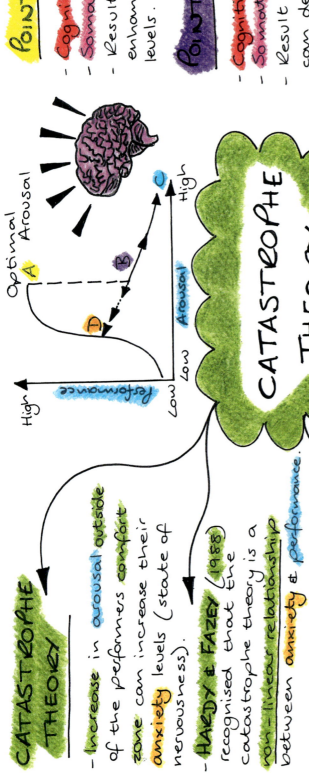

CATASTROPHE THEORY

- Increase in arousal outside of the performers comfort zone can increase their anxiety levels (state of nervousness).
- HARDY & FAZEY (1988) recognised that the catastrophe theory is a non-linear relationship between anxiety & performance.

- This theory recognises that continual mistakes made through a game/bout/event, lead to an increase in arousal, which in turn increases both...

- SOMATIC (physiological) and
- COGNITIVE (psychological) anxiety.

- As a result, this increase in anxiety (both types), leads to a CATASTROPHIC decline in performance.

CATASTROPHE THEORY

COGNITIVE ANXIETY (worry about performance) leads to high levels of

SOMATIC ANXIETY (struggling to perform skills correctly).

- eg A golfer plays a bad tee shot into the rough then continues to play bad shots subsequently, no matter what they do.

POINT A
- Cognitive anxiety is high
- Somatic anxiety is low
- Result = performance is enhanced, hitting optimal levels.

POINT B
- Cognitive anxiety is high
- Somatic anxiety is high
- Result = performance levels can decline (very, very quickly).

POINT D
- Performance does not return to original level straight away (even though the performer tries to reduce arousal).

POINT C
- Performance levels continue to decrease/deteriorate.

74

There are...

3 DIMENSIONS OF ANXIETY

- Cognitive
- Somatic
- Behavioural

& ...

2 TYPES OF ANXIETY

- Trait   ... to learn!
- State

ANXIETY

TYPES OF ANXIETY

SPIELBERGER (1966) suggested that there are 2 different types of anxiety.

TRAIT ANXIETY

- Innate levels of anxiety that form part of our 'personality'.
- Performers with high trait anxiety have a tendency to be fearful of unfamiliar situations & perceive competitive scenarios as threatening.
- AKA... Competitive trait anxiety (competition causes apprehension & tension).

STATE ANXIETY

- An emotional response to a particular situation - feel nervous & apprehensive.
- Often temporary & will depend on the performers interpretation of the stressfulness of the situation.
- Generally, people with high trait anxiety also have high state anxiety.
- eg Basketballer - comfortable in the game, however will suffer from high state anxiety at the free throw line, especially late in the game if the score is close.
- AKA... Competitive state anxiety.

LEVITT (1980) defines anxiety as ... 'the subjective feeling of apprehension and heightened psychological arousal often associated with fear, worries and doubts.'

THE THREE DIMENSIONS OF ANXIETY

SOMATIC

- Physiological response to a situation where the performer feels they may not cope.
- Tends to dissipate during a performance, therefore has minimal effect (for most performers).
- eg Increased heart rate, sweaty palms, muscle tension.

COGNITIVE

- Psychological response to a situation. Feelings of nervousness & apprehension.
- Irrational thinking & worries that may occur before & during a performance.
- 'fear of failure' / believing they do not have the ability.
- It is these negative thoughts that have the biggest negative impact on performance.

BEHAVIOURAL

- Feelings that lead to certain patterns of behaviours.
- Eg Biting fingernails, fidgeting, 'uncharacteristic behaviours' (can depend on their personality).

CATASTROPHE THEORY

Suggests...

- Stress & anxiety will influence performance.
- Each performer will respond in a unique way to competitive anxiety.
- Performance will be affected in an unique way & may be difficult to predict using general rules.
- As mentioned on page 47, this theory recognises that optimal mistakes made throughout a game lead to an increase in arousal.
- This in turn increases both SOMATIC (physiological) & COGNITIVE (psychological) anxiety.
- The graph below shows the relationship between cognitive & somatic anxiety. Increases in cognitive anxiety have a negative linear relationship with performance, whereas somatic anxiety tends to mimic the Inverted U hypothesis.

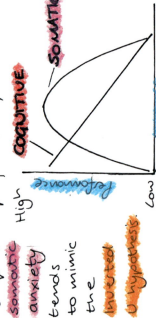

COGNITIVE / SOMATIC

Performance (Low–High) / Arousal (Low–High)

THE EFFECTS OF ANXIETY ON PERFORMANCE

3 to consider...
- Zone of Optimal functioning
- Catastrophe Theory
- Choking.

ZONE OF OPTIMAL FUNCTIONING

- Often referred to as... 'in the zone', 'state of flow', or 'peak flow experience', where performers feel they 'can do nothing wrong!'.
- When performers are in their optimal performance zone, this means they are experiencing their preferred level of anxiety & arousal.
- If a performer experiences too much or too little anxiety, this can hinder performance, as they are outside of their optimal zone.
- The 'zone of optimal functioning' is very individual & is experienced more regularly by expert/elite performers.

Maximum performance

Zone of optimal functioning

Performance (Low–High) / Arousal (Low–High)

CHOKING

- Refers to pervasive (common) problems in which there is a sudden impairment/failure of athletic performance due to anxiety.
- Characterised by cognitive anxiety & the feeling that 'the harder I try, the worse my performance.'
- Generally occurs on the 'big moment' or in 'big stage' or in high (mainly cognitive), which can increase anxiety systems & stress & lead to a bad performance, especially when arousal levels are high. Many, many eg's including Newcastle 1996 'losing' the Premier Leage to Man. Utd.

MEASURING ANXIETY

- You need to know the **ADVANTAGES** and **DISADVANTAGES** of different ways to measure **ANXIETY**, including...
  - **OBSERVATIONS**
  - **QUESTIONNAIRES**
  - **PHYSIOLOGICAL MEASURES**

QUESTIONNAIRES

- The **SPORT COMPETITIVE ANXIETY TEST (SCAT)**, or as it has evolved into the **COMPETITIVE SPORT ANXIETY INVENTORY (CSAI 2)** is a questionnaire that measures/assesses an individual's anxiety (both **COGNITIVE** & **SOMATIC**) & confidence levels.

- Has a maximum score of 36 & although it has no time limit, is recommended to be completed within an hour.

- Results are analysed by team psychologists & gives the coach an idea of the **anxiety** & confidence levels of their performers.

- This allows for the use of specific training scenarios & the application of appropriate strategies to decrease the negative impact of high levels of **cognitive anxiety** & low confidence can have on performance.

- Although quick to use & an immediate method to assess **anxiety** & confidence, they

- are not without their downfalls!

- Answers can differ depending when asked. eg. mood changes if win/lose.

- Questions may hold some bias.

- Questions could be specific & to the point; if long & boring performers may rush through.

- Questions should be easy to understand to allow realistic answers.

OBSERVATIONS

- Anxiety levels can be measured by watching a performer in training &/or a competitive environment.

- This has its advantages as the observer can see reactions & behaviour of a performer in real time in the environment they perform in.

- However, it has disadvantages as the observer will need to know what they are like in general to make accurate comparisons, as well as being well qualified (to make the judgements). This process can also be time consuming.

PHYSIOLOGICAL MEASURES

- Anxiety levels can be measured through identifying certain physiological responses to situations. eg. increased heart rate, breathing rate & sweating.

- Can be measured easily with technological advancements. eg. HR monitors & GPS data - give immediate factual data.

- However, certain responses could occur from being assessed (anticipatory rise) & fitness levels.

AGGRESSION & ASSERTION

CHANNELLED
- No intent to harm & within the rules & spirit of the game.
- Looking to play/compete within authority
- eg playing strong and powerful shots in tennis to score points quickly & finish off rallies on their own terms.

INSTRUMENTAL
- Aggressive behaviour that is inside the rules of the game, however is used to either cause harm, exploit weakness or intimidate.
- eg a cricket team may use a fast bowler to bowl short deliveries directed at the head/body to either intimidate or get them to play a bad shot (or set them up for another tactic).

AGGRESSION
- Is a term that is used in different ways, though it is important to distinguish between desirable and undesirable behaviours.
- BARON (1977) defines aggression as... 'any behaviour directed at the goal of harming or injuring another being who is motivated to avoid such treatment.'
eg punching someone in rugby.

TYPES OF AGGRESSION
- Hostile
- Channelled
- Reactive
- Instrumental

ASSERTION...
On the other hand is generally defined as...'forceful behaviour that is controlled and within the laws of the game.'
eg a perfectly timed tackle in rugby when contact is made around the waist & the tackler wins the collision.

REACTIVE
- Similar to hostile aggression, this also refers to aggressive behaviours that occur outside the rules of the game & with the intent to harm, but it is a reaction/retaliation to other aggressive acts.
- eg a high tackle in rugby results in a team mate hitting the opponent/instigator.

HOSTILE
- Refers to aggressive behaviours that occur outside the rules of the game & the intent to harm.
- eg a two footed tackle in football.

THEORIES OF AGGRESSION

FRUSTRATION-AGGRESSION HYPOTHESIS

- **DOLLARD (1939)** suggested that when a goal is blocked, frustration can occur, which in turn leads to aggressive behaviours.

- Closely linked to the Instinct Theory, once aggressive behaviours have been implemented, levels of frustration decrease, leading to **catharsis** (emotional release)

- This is only true if the act of aggression leads to success.

- If it is unsuccessful, more frustration can occur.

Catharsis ← Success

Drive → Obstacle → Frustration → Aggression
to goal

Punishment

SOCIAL LEARNING THEORY

- **BANDURA (1977)** believed that aggression is based on modelling/observing, which can in turn lead to behaviours being mimicked due to their experiences.

- This is why leaders & coaches have a duty to ensure rules are adhered to & any aggressive behaviours outside of the rules of the game are dealt with some type of consequence.

INSTINCT THEORY

- Proposed by **FREUD (1933)**, but researched further by **LORENZ** et al (1966).

- Suggests that aggression is genetically inherited & that we are biologically determined to act aggressively in an attempt to become dominant (though everyone has their own levels of **innate** aggression).

- **LORENZ** believed that aggressive energy can build up & needs to be released; sport can provide a 'perfect platform' for acceptable aggressive behaviour to be released.

AGGRESSIVE CUE HYPOTHESIS

- **BERKOWITZ (1969)** believed that frustration leads to an increase in arousal, but not immediate aggression.

- This depends on the situation & whether or not there are aggressive cues.

- if the sport lends itself to more aggressive acts (such as a collision sport like rugby league), then there is a greater chance of aggressive behaviour if frustration develops.

Frustration
eg blocking of a goal
→ Increased arousal
eg anger →
Presence of aggression → greater likelihood of aggression
no aggressive cues → less likelihood of aggression

STRATEGIES TO REDUCE AGGRESSION

- **Punishments.** This type of behaviour has consequences; fines, suspensions, loss of position on the team.

- **Encourage non-aggressive role models.**

- **Change position,** remove the aggressive player from the situation. eg substitute off.

- **Implement stress management** cognitive/relaxation techniques.

- **Use positive reinforcement for non-aggressive behaviour & negative reinforcement for aggressive behaviour.**

- **Look to change/modify the performers perception.** eg 'reframe' the situation.

- **Rewards given out now to highlight fair play.** eg the FIFA Fair Play Award.

LEARN...
- Aggression/Assertion
- Theories of Aggression
- Types of Aggression
- Causes of Aggression
- Strategies to reduce Aggression.

AGGRESSION

Bracketed morality. A temporary suspension during competition of the high level of ethical morality necessary for everyday life. i.e do not consider the needs/desires of anyone else due to the different environment the performer is in (on the pitch). Some performers may see the sporting arena as a 'different environment' to everyday life, so morals are different. eg politeness is not required, especially to the opposition, so sledging is ok!

CAUSES OF AGGRESSION

- **Nature of the game** (collision or contact) eg rugby league.

- **Hostile crowds** that increase arousal levels leading to aggressive behaviour. eg derby match in football.

- **Frustration.** Could be caused by poor performance, goals blocked, refereeing decisions, opposition (baiting/sledging).

- **Rivalry** eg The Ashes in cricket, Man Utd v Liverpool.

- **Reaction** to dirty play, provocation by opponent. eg Zidane in World Cup Final 2006.

- **Under developed moral reasoning.** The maturity of an athlete's moral reasoning can determine levels of aggressive behaviour. Some research suggests that some performers with lower moral reasoning are more likely to act aggressively & injure their opponent in their pursuit of success/goal.

- **'Win at all costs' attitude.**

... Why not?

NEGATIVE MOTIVATION

- This response is characterised by an improvement in performance out of a fear of not performing well.

- Although some type of negative motivation techniques may be needed in small doses (at elite level), some coaches use this too much & unfortunately negative motivation may decrease an athletes self-esteem & self-confidence.

- eg a player may train really hard, not for the sole reason of improving performance or fitness, but to reduce the chance of being yelled at or ridiculed by the coach!

INTRINSIC MOTIVATION

- The internal drive to succeed, where performers possess their own personal motivation, to have fun & enjoyment.

- A sense of pride by achieving a goal are also factors for high intrinsic levels of motivation. (intangible rewards such as recognition & sense of achievement).

- Making training fun & enjoyable as well as balancing the competitive aspect is key to success in sport.

- Generally usually based on higher levels of intrinsic motivation & closely linked to arousal levels. If a performer does not get the same enjoyment or sense of achievement as previously, arousal levels will not be in the optimum zone & so intrinsic motivation decreases.

MAEHR & ZUSHO (2009) define motivation as... 'the process that influences the initiation, direction, magnitude or intensity, perseverance, continuation and quality of a goal-directed behaviours.'

TYPES OF MOTIVATION

POSITIVE MOTIVATION

- Is a response that takes place when an individual's performance is driven by previous reinforcing behaviours.

- Relies on continual self reinforcement by external sources (such as coach, family, peers, spectators & the media).

- Positive motivation techniques can be used to enhance this response. eg clear communication, continual praise & encouragement.

EXTRINSIC MOTIVATION

- Extrinsic factors that drive a performer to succeed, or tangible rewards, such as money, trophies, big contracts as well as fame & pressure from other people.

- In the early or cognitive stage of learning, reinforcement through rewards & praise can be used to strengthen extrinsic motivation.

- However, this must be balanced carefully with intrinsic motivation as the performer progresses through the stages of learning.

- eg a Tour de France cyclist may be motivated to win the race & the fame that comes with it (extrinsic motivation & extrinsic reward) but can also gain satisfaction & enjoyment from the task (intrinsic motivation & intrinsic reward).

IN SHORT... 'motivation has two aspects: it is what drives us to do things... and makes us do particular things.' WOODS (1998)

Motivation has 2 main dimensions; intensity & direction.

INTENSITY - is concerned with arousal, which determines the amount of effort that is given to achieving a set of goals... DIRECTION.

81

THEORIES OF MOTIVATION

NACH - NEED TO ACHIEVE

- The people have 'approach behaviours' & tend to seek challenging situations.
- The performers are not afraid of failure & seek criticism in order to improve performance.
- They set high goals & take risks in the pursuit of success or improvement in standard.

- However, there is a high value to success.
- A boxer with a NACH personality type may approach this challenge as they do not fear failure & are motivated to succeed.
- On the flip side for the heavy-weight champion, there is a high probability of success, but little value & satisfaction to be gained from winning, as it is expected.
- Therefore there will be little motivation to take on this bout, especially if they are more intrinsically motivated an extrovert.

ACHIEVEMENT MOTIVATION

- Achievement motivation has 2 dimensions...

  NAF - Need to Avoid Failure w
  NACH - Need to Achieve w

ATKINSON & McCLELLAND

- ATKINSON & McCLELLAND (1953) both proposed that achievement motivation comes from the individual's personality & it is their motivation to strive for success.

- The concept links personality to competitiveness.

  ACHIEVEMENT MOTIVATION = INTRINSIC MOTIVATION

  - COGNITIVE STATE ANXIETY

FACTORS THAT INFLUENCE BEHAVIOUR

- SITUATIONAL FACTORS - affect motivation for performance, generally influenced by the probability of success or failure & the rewards that can be gained as a result.

- eg if there is a difficult task (beating the heavyweight champion in boxing), there is a low probability of success for a new heavyweight boxer.

NAF - NEED TO AVOID FAILURE

- These people have 'avoidance behaviours' & are intent on avoiding competitive situations.

- Performers with NAF personalities/ personality types have low need to achieve, fear failure & lack a competitive edge (this could be due to learned helplessness)

- Performers will generally select low goals (as this will give them some kind of achievement) or very high goals (as the expectation of them succeeding is low).

- However, praise may be awarded for attempting such a situation (heroic failure syndrome).

82

ACHIEVEMENT GOAL THEORY

- NACH = NEED TO ACHIEVE.

- If a coach would like to develop more approach behaviours for his/her team or an individual, they could consider the following strategies.

- Adjust the way they set goals. Rather than focussing on outcome goals, a more task orientated approach could be set, allowing success in small steps.

- Reinforcement. Positive praise when elements of performance or task have been completed well or have been successful.

- Attribution. Ensuring that success is attributed to internal factors, (such as ability & effort)

STRATEGIES TO DEVELOP APPROACH BEHAVIOURS

- Leading to improvements in performance.

- Approach behaviours are associated with performers NACH personality types.

ACHIEVEMENT GOAL THEORY

ACHIEVEMENT GOAL THEORY

- Suggests that motivation & task persistence depend on the type of goals set & how they will measure success.

OUTCOME ORIENTATED GOALS

- Focus around what the ultimate result is (i.e whether they win or lose).

- They do not take into account the process of the performance.

- If the performer succeeds, then there is satisfaction.

- However, if the performer fails, confidence levels decrease.

TASK ORIENTATED GOALS

- Are more concerned with the process & improving performance in a task, not necessarily winning as the ultimate outcome.

- Even if the performer does not succeed in terms of the outcome, but improves performance confidence is maintained as they achieved the task set.

- Modify training. Ensure success is achievable in training, even if it means going 'back to basics'.

- Performance accomplishments (self efficacy). Use positive & successful past performances to improve the confidence of the performer.

The effect of
Social
Facilitation

Performance (High → Low) vs Arousal (Low → High) graph

SOCIAL FACILITATION

- Refers to <u>how</u> the presence of an audience/crowd positively enhances performance.

SOCIAL INHIBITION

- Refers to the negative effect on performance due to the attendance of an audience/crowd.

- ZAJONC (1965) found that the mere presence of others is sufficient to increase the arousal levels of a performer.
Linking closely with the DRIVE THEORY (P.72). He grouped the 'others' into 2 categories...

PASSIVE
INTERACTIVE

PASSIVE

- Audience & co-actors.
- Does <u>not</u> have a big influence on performance compared to interactive others...

INTERACTIVE

- Competitors & spectators.
- Has a greater impact on performance.

- Competitors can directly influence a performance physically & spectators can increase arousal levels.
- This is especially true if the crowd is close to play (proximity effect) & playing away from home.

As arousal increases, there is a greater likelihood of the DOMINANT RESPONSE occurring. In the case of an elite performer, the dominant response is more than likely to be the correct one, improving performance (SOCIAL FACILITATION).

HOWEVER

- For a performer in the early/cognitive stage of learning, the DOMINANT RESPONSE is likely to be incorrect.
- This will therefore have an adverse & detrimental effect on performance (SOCIAL INHIBITION). It may reflect a negative line & some of the information with regards the INVERTED U HYPOTHESIS (see page 73) will/may apply.

- The same concept applies to fine & complex skills being performed in the presence of others.
The increased levels of arousal will increase the likelihood of an incorrect execution.
- ...whereas the performance of simple & gross skills will increase the likelihood of a correct response & positive execution.

- Unless the performer feels that one of the passive others is significant/significant to them & they have the feeling they may be assessed.
- Leads to higher anxiety levels.

SOCIAL FACILITATION & INHIBITION

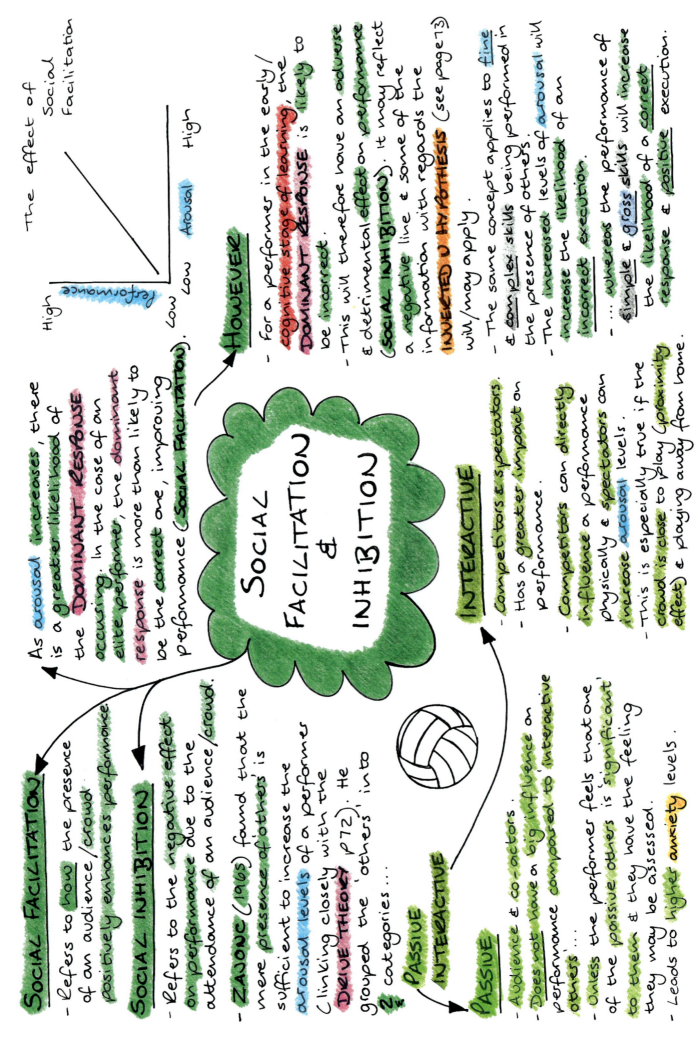

84

SOCIAL FACILITATION & INHIBITION

EVALUATION APPREHENSION

- COTTRELL (1968) suggested that it is not the presence of others that leads to an increase in arousal, it is whether or not the performer perceives that the audience/crowd is assessing or judging their performance.

- eg a young netballer may be calm with an audience watching her play.

- However, if there were scouts present evaluating her performance, then her **arousal levels & anxiety** levels could increase ... as a result of EVALUATION APPREHENSION.

STRATEGIES TO MINIMISE SOCIAL INHIBITION

- Practice selective attention
- Use imagery &/or mental rehearsal to block out the audience/crowd.
- Ensure skills over-learnt.
- Introduce evaluative others into practice - allows performer to get used to the process.
- Appropriate use of attribution
- Stress management techniques in training.
- Greater awareness of appropriate arousal levels & zone of optimal functioning.

EFFECTS ON PERFORMANCE
of Social Facilitation

- It is no surprise that most teams playing at home have a higher win percentage than those playing away.
- This can mainly be attributed to familiar surroundings & a more supportive home crowd.

- However, this could work against the home team if they are on a 'losing streak', or in tight situations (close result), that could ultimately lead to 'choking'. (see page 76)

- The PROXIMITY EFFECT can also affect **arousal & anxiety** levels. Sports such as basketball & netball have crowds that are very close to the action, creating a more hostile environment for the away team.

- ... whereas some football & rugby stadia (mainly newer grounds) set crowds back from the action

- The recent Coronavirus pandemic has negated this home advantage with games being played for large chunks of time behind closed doors.

Presence of others → Arousal → Dominant Response

If Dominant response is incorrect → Process loss

If Dominant Response is correct → Process gain

GROUP DYNAMICS

GROUP FORMATION

- The first 4 stages of team growth were initially developed by BRUCE TUCKMAN (1965).
- Tuckman's model helps to explain that these stages were an inevitable & important part of the process if a team was to grow to a point where it could function together effectively & deliver results!

- Not every team will make it to this final stage (stage 4).
- Some teams get stuck on the storming or norming stage.
- Factors that can affect this include...
  - size of group (if too big can be hard to define individual roles)
  - personalities
  - coaching styles
  - goals (individual goals may conflict with team goals).

STAGE 1 - FORMING

- Takes place when the team first meets each other & they get a feel of the team environment.
- Training not yet started.
- Team members share information about interests, experiences etc & form first impressions of each other.
- Plans for the year with regards to goals, training & competition are discussed.

STAGE 2 - STORMING

- Team members compete for status, acceptance of their ideas & positions within the team.
- Can lead to conflict.
- This stage is unavoidable & every team, especially a new one, will go through this phase of development.

STAGE 3 - NORMING

- After initial conflict, boundaries are set & all issues resolved.
- The team starts to work together, with team members beginning to trust each other.
- They are not competing against each other, they are helping each other work towards a common goal.

STAGE 4 - PERFORMING

- The team is now working at a high level & they all know their roles.
- Team members have gotten to know each other, trust each other & rely on each other.
- The likelihood of successful performance is higher once this stage is reached.

GROUP & TEAM DYNAMICS

CARRON'S FOUR FACTORS OF GROUP COHESION.

ENVIRONMENTAL FACTORS.
- Factors that help bind groups together include age, location, employment & ethos.
- Holding camps, equal importance & value amongst the group can improve group cohesion.

PERSONAL FACTORS.
- Refers to the belief in the group, a desire to win & social relationships within community/group.
- Desire to achieve excellence generally shared & it is important in avoiding the formation of cliques.

LEADERSHIP FACTORS.
- The influence of the coach or manager is important in building identity.
- Leaders can improve cohesion by affiliation through task & social cohesion factors (eg Sir Alex Ferguson, Pep Guardiola).

TEAM FACTORS.
- The team or group should have a clear identity, with set targets & every member of that group feeling that they have a role in the team.

There are 2 theories to consider with regard to group/team dynamics. These are...

- Carson
- Steiner

Plus Ringlemann effect

A GROUP
- SHAW (1976) defines a group as... 'two or more people interacting with one another in a manner that each person influences and is influenced by each other person.'

GROUP DYNAMICS
- Refers to ... 'the processes operating within the group' between individual members.

- CARRON (1980) stated that a cohesive group will have the following characteristics...
  - a collective identity
  - a sense of shared purpose
  - structured patterns of communication

TASK COHESION
- The way team members work together to successfully complete a task.
- eg all working together to complete a set penalty corner tactic in hockey successfully.

SOCIAL COHESION
- The interaction & relationship within a group.
- eg having a strong bond during the Olympic period or on a cricket tour will improve group cohesion.

STEINER & RINGELMANN EFFECT

STRATEGIES TO DEVELOP GROUP COHESION

- Holding training camps to build unity.
- Ensure all members of the group have equal value & importance.
- rewarding all players equally with praise/criticism
- mixing young/old together
- developing a shared responsibility for (players), or different subgroups.
- avoiding the formation of cliques.
- identifying why members individually want to be part of the group (building on their motives).
- identifying those who exhibit 'social loafing' & introduce methods to incorporate them into the group
- unite players in their belief of the leader.
- through leadership style & behaviour (mix of autocratic/democratic - more later on page).
- incorporate a 'leadership group' that is approachable for players.
- avoid criticising individuals in front of the group. Be aware of each the team.
- get to know players needs & their preferred way of interacting & style of motivation.
- Appropriate use of team goals in the short, medium & big term.
- clear member roles in the group as integral to the team ethic (avoid Ringlemann effect).

LOSSES DUE TO FAULTY PROCESSES (FP)
- factors that can go wrong in team performance which impede group cohesion.

POTENTIAL PRODUCTIVITY (PP)
- The maximum capability of the group when cohesiveness is strongest.

ACTUAL PRODUCTIVITY (AP)
- The team performance at any given time (due to successful interaction).

STEINER
- Group cohesion is the force that binds a group together, helping prevent faulty processes (ie losses due to poor form, reduced motivation & lack of teamwork).
- A team full of great individuals is not always the best formula, especially if there are faulty processes that lead to a lack of cohesion.
- for STEINER (1972), in order for a group to perform to their Potential, essential team strategies need to be implemented that maintain motivation & improve group productivity & also reduce the chance of SOCIAL LOAFING.
  motivation loss due to SOCIAL LOAFING.

RINGELMANN EFFECT & SOCIAL LOAFING
According to RINGELMANN (1974) when working in groups, an individuals performance will decrease. why?
- Co-ordination losses where 'operational effectiveness' of the group cannot be sustained for the whole match. eg lineout execution wrong due to bad timing of jump & positional issues.
- Co-ordination problems more likely as size of group increases.

- Motivation losses can also lead to lack of effort, especially in a big group (not everyone has a defined role).
- Individuals may think others will 'pick up the slack' - this is known as SOCIAL LOAFING
- devise & identify a clear system of rewards & punishments - group help devise.
- encourage social bonding through social events.

GOAL SETTING

SHORT-TERM
- In order to achieve a LONG term goal, a series of short term goals should be set, or goals that have been periodised.
- eg a netballer will periodise her training & have a separate focus for each phase of training to achieve peak fitness at certain times.

MEDIUM-TERM
- Goals set at certain points to encourage & maintain motivation. Particularly important for Olympic athletes or for sports with a long season.
- eg an Olympic athlete may have a medium term goal of winning a national competition before setting their sights on the long term goal of Olympic Gold!

LONG-TERM
- Ultimate goals to achieve at the end of a training programme or what you are in pursuit of.
- eg lose 1 kg after a 16 week training programme or to win Gold at the next Olympic Games.

TYPES OF GOALS TO OPTIMISE PERFORMANCE

Goals can be...
- SUBJECTIVE
- OBJECTIVE
- OUTCOME
- PERFORMANCE
- PROCESS
- REALISTIC & ASPIRATIONAL

& set in the SHORT, MEDIUM & LONG TERM.

FOR ATTENTIONAL FOCUS
- Allows performers to focus on the important factors & cues in order to improve performance.

PERSISTENCE ON TASKS
- Setting goals can motivate performers to continue in their 'pursuit of perfection' of a certain skill, task or to improve an area of weakness.

RAISING CONFIDENCE & SELF EFFICACY
- Setting performance (improving end performance) & process (usually part of a performance/skill) goals with incremental steps can allow a performer to gradually gain confidence in certain situations.
- This will eventually lead to a better overall level of performance.

CONTROL OF AROUSAL & ANXIETY
- Setting goals will not only assist in improving confidence & motivation but it will increase the chances of controlling arousal & anxiety (optimal arousal zone).

MONITOR PERFORMANCE
- Goals can be broken down into short, medium & long-term.
- Progress can be measured though out a training programme.
- This will in turn increase motivation & lead to greater progress being made.

IMPORTANCE & EFFECTIVENESS
of goal setting. Why set them?

89

GOAL SETTING & MOTIVATION

There are 4 main types of goals to learn for developing & enhancing motivation
- Mastery
- Outcome
- Socially approved
- Task orientated

OUTCOME GOALS
- ... sometimes called

EGO GOALS.
- Motivated by winning.
- These type of goals are only recommended for the 'elite-performes' in top level competitions, & not for performers in the early/ cognitive stage of learning.

SOCIALLY APPROVED GOALS
- These goals are set to improve on weaknesses in performance.
- Seek to get external approval & reinforcement to help increase motivation.
- eg receiving positive reinforcement from a captain or coach that you have performed your role in a 'set play/move' correctly.

TASK ORIENTATED GOALS
- Desire to win
- ... however the process is about perfecting certain tasks within a performance as a way of improving performance overall (in the long run).
- eg improving 1st serve success rate in tennis will lead to greater performance overall.

MASTERY GOALS
- ... or PROCESS GOALS.
- Can be used to help set targets for improvement in a performance.
- These goals are not necessarily focussed on the overall result.
- They are more about achieving & mastering goals that are broken down in order to eventually achieve an overall goal.
- Generally associated with mastering a technical element.
- eg (improving a certain aspect of performance) such as the technical efficiency of a somersault within a trampolining routine.

GOAL SETTING
- There is more about goal setting later in the book (page 62-3), focussed on the SMARTER principle & their use, importance & effectiveness in optimising performance.

TYPES OF GOALS

OUTCOME

- Also known as **PRODUCT** goals.
- Focus on achieving success in a competitive situation (game, tournament, competition).
- The target (goal) is based on the <u>end result</u> & is concerned with the outcome of the competition.

PERFORMANCE RELATED

- Goals that focus on achieving standards based on <u>performance</u> & improving on previous performances, <u>not</u> in comparison to others.
- Provide 'stepping stones' to improve the overall outcome.
- Enhance **motivation & confidence**.
- eg improving an overhead clear in badminton in order to force the opponent to the back of the court, to establish a better position to play more attacking shots.

PROCESS

- Focus on specific actions that need to be achieved during a performance & are mainly focussed on a specific <u>skill/technique</u>.
- eg improving tumble turns in swimming in order to improve the overall outcome goal of winning the race.

SUBJECTIVE

- Are goals based on opinions & feelings?
- Are they general ≠ generic?
- Goals should be <u>specific</u> with <u>clear</u> targets.
- ... however, activities such as dance & gymnastics may have more subjective goals, based on the subjective nature of how the quality of performance is assessed.

REALISTIC & ASPIRATIONAL

- Goals should be **realistic** (in that they can be achieved)
- ... however they must also be **aspirational** & challenging to motivate & inspire a performer to train hard to accomplish the overall goal.
- The performer therefore will be more likely to maintain **motivation** & continue with their training.

OBJECTIVE

- These goals can be measured with **quantifiable** data.
- eg training logs, notational data, video analysis, fitness tests.
- These types of goals make it much easier to track & monitor progress made by the performer.

GOAL SETTING

The **SMART(ER)** principle should be used for goal setting. This stands for

- **S**PECIFIC
- **M**EASUREABLE
- **A**CHIEVABLE
- **R**EALISTIC
- **T**IME-BOUND
- **E**VALUATE
- **R**E-DO

SPECIFIC

- Goals must be clear & relevant to the performer and any weaknesses noticeable in performance.

- They should also include specific targets that allow them to be measured against certain/set criteria.

MEASUREABLE

- The use of data to measure progress (or a lack of it!), assist in developing motivation, or to allow the performer & coach to make adjustments if required.

ACHIEVABLE

- Similar to Realistic, so AGREED is probably a more suitable term to use.

- In order for goals to be effective, all parties involved (performer & coach) must be in agreement that the goals set are challenging, but also realistic based on the performers ability.

REALISTIC

- Results of tests & others monitoring aspects of a goal should be recorded to allow the performer & coach to reflect on progress. Achieving certain step-by-step goals can increase performer motivation to continue to improve.

TIME-BOUND

- Goals are best achieved when staggered over a training year.

- Elite performers/teams tend to set goals each training cycle (or through their periodised plan), in order to maintain motivation & make training more realistic & achievable.

EVALUATE

- Setting goals & targets allows the performer to evaluate progress & make adjustments along the way.
- E can also stand for EXCITING.

- By making goals exciting in pursuit of achieving something the performer really wants to accomplish, it can increase motivation & keep the performer on track.

RE-DO

- If the goal has not been achieved or progress has stalled, then the performer should attempt the plan again.

- The performer should think about what has gone wrong & adjust the goal according to the weakness. May include adjusting the target(s).

WEINER'S MODEL OF ATTRIBUTION

- WEINER (1974) identified
  - Ability
  - Effort
  - Task Difficulty
  - Luck

... as the most important factors affecting achievement

- It has **3** main dimensions...
  - Causality
  - Stability
  - Controllability

Causality
Internal | External

| Ability | Task Difficulty |
| Effort | Luck |

Stability
stable / unstable

WEINER'S ATTRIBUTION THEORY

LOCUS OF CAUSALITY

- This dimension is mainly linked to whether the attributions are internal (with performers) or external, eg environmental.

- Ability & effort are seen as internal factors.

- Task difficulty & luck are seen as external factors (outside the control of the performer).

STABILITY

- Is referring to whether the reasons/causes were relatively permanent (stable) or changeable (unstable) in relation to time.

- Ability & task difficulty are seen as being stable factors (in relation to time).

- Effort & luck are changeable, therefore seen as unstable.

ATTRIBUTION THEORY

- Seeks to explain how individuals & teams elevate their levels of success & failure.

- It also seeks to show how the reasons given by an individual or team, or how they perceive their success or failure, may affect future motivation in similar situations.

CONTROLLABILITY

- Helps to explain the effective consequences of attributions that appear to be in a person's control (or not).

- This dimension has been shown to relate to the intensity of a performers personal feeling of satisfaction & pride, shame & guilt.

- Motivation, pride etc will increase if a performer relates their success to internal causes (eg ability & effort), rather than external uncontrollable factors.

- The opposite effect will generally occurs if failure is also attributed to internal & controllable factors.

- Shame, dissatisfaction & loss of motivation are likely.

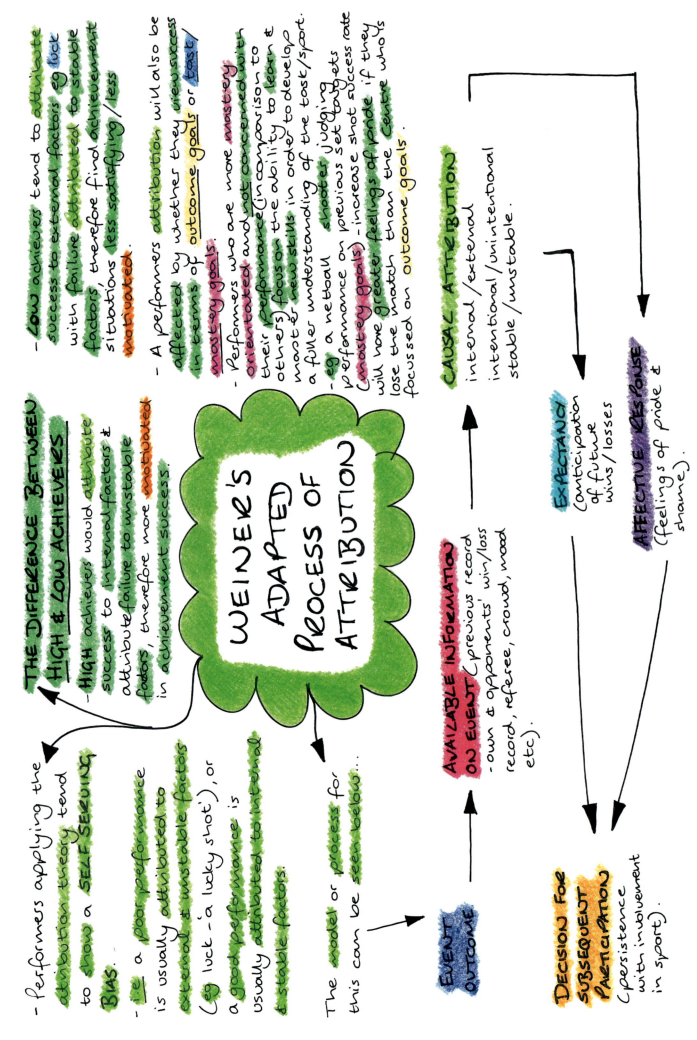

THE DIFFERENCE BETWEEN HIGH & LOW ACHIEVERS

- HIGH achievers would attribute success to internal factors & attribute failure to unstable factors, therefore more **motivated** in achievement success.

- Low achievers tend to attribute success to external factors eg luck with failure attributed to stable factors, therefore find achievement situations 'less satisfying/less **motivated**.

- A performers attribution will also be affected by whether they view success in terms of **outcome goals** or **task**.

- A performers attribution will also be affected by whether they view success in terms of **mastery goals**.

- Performers who are more **mastery** orientated and not concerned with their performance (in comparison to others) focus on the ability to learn & master new skills in order to develop a fuller understanding of the test/sport.

- eg a netball shooter judging performance on previous set targets (mastery goals) - increase shot success rate will have greater feelings of pride if they lose the match than the centre who's focussed on outcome goals.

- Performers applying the attribution theory tend to show a **SELF SERVING** Bias.

- ie a poor performance is usually attributed to external & unstable factors (eg luck - 'a lucky shot'), or a good performance is usually attributed to internal & stable factors.

The model or process for this can be seen below...

CAUSAL ATTRIBUTION
internal/external
intentional/unintentional
stable/unstable.

EXPECTANCY
(anticipation of future wins/losses)

AFFECTIVE RESPONSE
(feelings of pride & shame).

WEINER'S ADAPTED PROCESS OF ATTRIBUTION

AVAILABLE INFORMATION ON EVENT (previous record - own & opponents' win/loss record, referee, crowd, mood etc).

EVENT OUTCOME

DECISION FOR SUBSEQUENT PARTICIPATION
(persistence with involvement in sport).

ATTRIBUTIONAL RE-TRAINING

... is called ATTRIBUTION RE-TRAINING

- This is a very important responsibility of the coach/teacher.

- Getting performers to realise that failure is *not* inevitable & teaching them *how to make* appropriate attributions with regard to their performance, *especially* when they are possibly already experiencing 'learned helplessness'.

- To help with **motivation**, a lack of success should be attributed to aspects that are *within the control of the performer*, such as inconsistent technique, lack of experience, bad tactical decisions etc.

The **model** or **process** for **'re-attribution'** can be seen below.

- Certain strategies such as ...

- Focussing on **mastery/task goals**
- Individual attention
- Having a positive outlook

... *can all assist* in the 're-attribution process.

NEGATIVE PERFORMANCE

Change to a positive outcome

Attribution - incorrect strategy was selected

Change strategy for the next fixture - create positive feelings for future success in performance.

Attribution - lack of ability

Make a connection between success of other performers tactics/strategies & your future performance.

Change from a negative response

Emotion becomes negative. *eg* frustration

Behaviour of learned helplessness

PERFORMANCE ACCOMPLISHMENTS

- High levels of previous success will lead to high self efficacy (& vice versa).

- Coaches & teachers must balance their sessions as some learners/ performers may not have experienced any success before so differentiated goals may need to be set.

VICARIOUS EXPERIENCES

- Watching others, especially of a similar ability succeed in sport will give the observer higher self efficacy & the feeling they can succeed.

- eg. if a student is reluctant to join a basketball club, but observes a friend performing well in a session, he/she is more likely to join in.

VERBAL PERSUASION

- A message from a significant other, ie. a respected leader is more likely to increase self efficacy as long as the message is believable & inspiring.

- If not, then the message is ignored & there is no (positive) effect on self confidence.

Efficacy Expectations → Athletic Performance

- Performance Accomplishments
- Vicarious Experiences
- Verbal Persuasion
- Emotional Arousal

SELF EFFICACY

SELF EFFICACY

- ... is defined as 'the level of self confidence in any given situation or situational specific self confidence.'

- BANDURA (1977) identified 4 key factors in the development of self efficacy & the expectation for future success.

LEARNED HELPLESSNESS

It is an acquired state related to the performers perceptions that they have no control over the situation, with failure/defeat being inevitable.

Characteristics include...

- specific to one activity or general (global) to all activities.
- performers usually outcome orientated
- from previous bad experiences.
- perceptions of low ability
- rarely tries new skills
- initial failure of new skills confirms perceptions.
- feelings of embarrassment.
- future effort limited
- lacks motivation
- feels incompetent.

EMOTIONAL AROUSAL

- If the performer feels under aroused, then they will lack confidence.

- Being in the optimum arousal zone will increase confidence.

- This will ultimately lead to an improvement in performance.

VEALEY'S MODEL OF SPORT-SPECIFIC CONFIDENCE

A sporting example (basketball free throw) will be used to outline Vealey's model.

THE SPORT SITUATION

- Shooting a free throw

TRAIT SPORTS CONFIDENCE

- This is the **innate** level of confidence (natural) possessed & is relatively stable.
- Relates to general ability to succeed in all sporting activities.

COMPETITIVE ORIENTATION

- Extent to which the performer is prepared to compete to succeed.
- 'Do you want to get the shot in because you want to win or just add to your statistics?'.

STATE SPORTS CONFIDENCE

- Can be developed through learning & is **unstable**.
- Relates to the belief about ability to succeed in a particular sport or situation in a sport. eg confidence in shooting a free throw.
- influenced by trait sports confidence & performers competitive orientation

PERFORMANCE

- Execution of the free throw.

SUBJECTIVE OUTCOME

- Perception of the outcome of the skill through feedback (internal & external).
- If the performer perceives the outcome was successful, this will increase **trait sports** confidence, competitiveness & **state** sports confidence. The opposite will occur if the outcome is perceived as negative.

SELF-CONFIDENCE

- is defined as ... 'the sureness or degree of certainty of feeling that you are equal to the task or challenge.'

VEALEY'S MODEL

- VEALEY (1986) proposed a sport specific theory of confidence and defined sport confidence as ...

'the belief or degree of certainty individuals possess about their ability to be successful in sport.

IMPACT OF SPORTS CONFIDENCE

PERFORMANCE

- Having **high levels** of sports confidence will generally lead to **greater motivation** to achieve success (both within training and competition/games).

PARTICIPATION

- High levels of **self confidence** enables the individual to be able to **integrate** more within team activities & not feel apprehensive in their ability to contribute.

SELF-ESTEEM

- Performers with high levels of **self confidence** will often have high levels of **self esteem**. This helps to reduce **anxiety** levels for optimal **arousal** that can potentially improve performance.

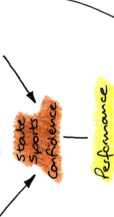

Competitive Orientation

The Sport Situation eg free throw

State Sports Confidence

Performance

Subjective Outcome

Trait Sport Confidence

97

STRATEGIES TO DEVELOP HIGH LEVELS OF SELF EFFICACY

GOAL SETTING

- Ensure goals follow the SMARTER method (see pg 2) with performers having some input/ownership of the goals set, as well as encourage-ment in the fact that the goals are realistic and achievable.

DEMONSTRATIONS

- Especially important for novice performers, they will require accurate visual demonstrations to build a mental picture of how to perform a certain skill.

- This should ultimately lead to greater confidence & higher rates of success.

SUCCESS IN TRAINING

- Structure sessions in a way that allows performers to achieve some success & develop intensity or level of difficulty in a more progressive way.

ATTRIBUTION

- Ensuring that any success is attributed to internal factors (ability, effort) & to then attribute failure to factors such as luck & task difficulty.

ENCOURAGEMENT

- Constant praise & reinforcement will help performers become more comfortable about their performance, especially with success.

AIM - LEADING TO IMPROVEMENTS IN PERFORMANCE

AROUSAL AND ANXIETY CONTROL

- Coaches can help performers understand their emotions, how to control arousal & anxiety through stress management techniques & to recognise their zone of optimal functioning through varying experiences.

PERFORMANCE ACCOMPLISHMENTS

- Use positive and successful past performances to improve confidence of the performer.

LEADERSHIP STYLES

3 to consider...

AUTOCRATIC

- Take control & dictate the rules & expectations
- Seen more when teaching *novice athletes* & when a decision is needed quickly in a dangerous situation or game saving scenario.
- *Not recommended for elite performers* as creativity & freedom of expression (of their talents) will be hampered.

DEMOCRATIC

- 'Person related' leadership style.
- Strong inter-personal skills.
- Leader listens to opinions of the group & shares the decision making process.
- Leader still has/makes the final decision when required.
- Most leaders apply all styles, though a more *democratic* approach has been the *most* consistent.

Leaders can be a combination of *EMERGENT* & *PRESCRIBED*.
eg team captain selected by the coach & also voted in by the players.

CHARACTERISTICS OF EFFECTIVE LEADERS

There is *no* single quality or clear guidelines on what the specific qualities of an effective leader are.

- ...however the factors listed below are seen to be most important.
  - *Motivated* & enthusiastic
  - Sport specific skills & knowledge (generally played at the same/similar level.)
  - Respect & empathy
  - Good interpersonal skills
  - Charismatic
  - Consistency & fairness
  - Clear vision & goals.

LAISSEZ-FAIRE

- Little direction or decisions made by the leader.
- Often made by the team.
- Not seen in action too much, though some aspects *can* *increase motivation* - feel they can be trusted. Will only work with an experienced group.

Leaders can be...

PRESCRIBED

- Selected for the position by an external body eg senior committee at a rugby club appoint from outside the organisation.
- Usually done when an 'overhaul' or change is *needed* within the set up.
- Has the advantage of coming in with *fresh ideas* & an *unbiased* view.
- ...However, group cohesion may suffer in the short term, due to unfamiliarity with the team culture & new working relationships.

Or... EMERGENT

- Emerges from within the group/team
- Selected by their *peers* due to their leadership character-istics. eg the next team captain.
- Generally the most successful leaders, as they have the *support* & respect of the team.
- However, they may not view aspects of the game objectively (or the team), leading to bias in selection due to friendship groups.

99

LEADER CHARACTERISTICS

- Refers to how experienced the leader is & the **personality** of the leader.
- i.e has the leader got the experience to deal with a group in a dangerous situation?

ACTUAL BEHAVIOUR considers what the leader actually decides to do.

- eg a more **autocratic** style as an experienced leader would increase trust from the group, as they know it is of benefit to listen to the leader.

MEMBER CHARACTERISTICS

- Refers to the <u>age & experience</u> of the group. i.e a group of 10yr old students will generally be inexperienced in more dangerous activities.

PREFERRED BEHAVIOUR refers to the <u>style</u> of leadership favoured by the group.
Continuing with the theme of dangerous activities, the group would prefer a more **autocratic** style of leadership, as the leader is telling them exactly what to do & they feel safe with this.

* If required/preferred & actual behaviour match, both performance & satisfaction increases.

CHELLADURI'S MODEL OF LEADERSHIP

To assess the effectiveness of leadership, behaviours must be analysed. *

CONSEQUENCES

7. Performance
Satisfaction.

LEADER BEHAVIOUR

4. Required Behaviours
5. Actual Behaviours
6. Preferred Behaviours

ANTECEDENTS

1. Situational Characteristics
2. Leader Characteristics
3. Member Characteristics

* If required & actual behaviour match, performance increases.

* If preferred & actual behaviour match, satisfaction increases.

MULTI-DIMENSIONAL MODEL

CHELLADURI (1990) identified **3** variables or antecedents that influence leadership. They are...

SITUATIONAL CHARACTERISTICS

- Environmental circumstances i.e is the activity dangerous?

REQUIRED BEHAVIOUR refers to the most suitable behaviours by the leader.
i.e is the leader experienced in the size of a group, tasks etc).

- In the case of the activity being dangerous, an **autocratic** leadership style would be best suited.

THEORIES OF LEADERSHIP

TRAIT PERSPECTIVE

- Leadership qualities are innate & genetically inherited.
- 'You either a born leader or not.' (NATURE).
- The early thinking behind the instinct theory was called 'THE GREAT MAN THEORY', where leaders are men as they are born with the relevant personality traits to be an effective leader.
- However, this theory fails to take into account any situational, environmental & interaction factors.

SOCIAL LEARNING

- Leadership qualities are learnt from others through observation & modelling (NURTURE).
- This learning process is strengthened if it is observed from a significant other (someone the person respects or someone of a higher status).

INTERACTIONIST

- Possess certain innate leadership traits, but only demonstrate these in specific (state) situations.
- Interaction of traits & dynamic environment.

Central: FIEDLER'S CONTINGENCY MODEL & THEORIES

SITUATIONAL VARIABLES

LEADERSHIP STYLES ⟷ RELATIONSHIP BETWEEN STYLES & SITUATION ⟷ SITUATIONAL VARIABLES

FIEDLER (1967) identified 2 styles of leadership...
- TASK ORIENTATED
- PERSON ORIENTATED

TASK ORIENTATED

- This style of leadership is concerned about achieving a particular outcome i.e winning.
- There are clear goals.
- Would suit a more autocratic leader.
- Generally has the greatest success in the most & least favourable scenarios.

PERSON ORIENTATED

- Concerned with the personal relationships & building strong (group) cohesion.
- Generally works with a more experienced group where a more democratic leader would be suitable & where opinions are valued.
- This leadership style has most success in moderately favourable scenarios.

STRESS MANAGEMENT

STRESSOR

- A stressor is something that causes stress and can include the following examples in sport...

- Playing in a high stakes match or event.
  - eg FA Cup Final.

- Competing against the best team/ performers in the sport.

- The need to play well to be selected for a representative team, or to secure a new contract.

- 'Fear of failure' & possessing NAF style personality traits.

- Injury or first competitive involvement since an injury.

- Effects of the crowd & pressure to win.

- stressors are... conflict, competitive, personal, frustration, audience, physiological & climatic.

STRESS

- Stress is a negative response to the body to a threat that causes anxiety.

- Eustress is a positive response to the body to a threat (ie the positive good feeling felt by a performer from a threatening situation).
  - eg: successfully skiing down a steep off piste run & overcoming the threatening challenge.

USE OF A WARM UP

- To aid stress management.

- A warm up, or Pre-Performance routine (PPR), can provide a performer with a coping strategy, by providing familiarity & control through the use of a pre-planned routine.

- Most people think that a warm up is used only to prepare the body for physiological responses.

- However, a gradual increase in HR & breathing pattern can help to regulate arousal, improve confidence & reduce the chance of choking.

COGNITIVE STRESS MANAGEMENT TECHNIQUES

MENTAL REHEARSAL / VISUALISATION

- Creating mental pictures of specific movements/actions executed in an actual game/event is a way of preparing for competition, reducing stress & making the performer feel more relaxed & prepared.
- Using mental pictures & specific sounds (of game/event) can create more realistic/vivid mental images.

IMAGERY

- Mental imagery can help with confidence & focus and at the same time, reduce anxiety.
- More experienced performers can use images of past performances (where they have been successful) to prepare & reinforcing their ability to perform well.
- Leads to an increase in confidence.

GOAL SETTING

- Setting clear goals can help a performer re-focus away from the source of stress & focus on more processes & performance goals.
- Setting realistic & achieveable goals can help to alleviate & reduce stress.

NEGATIVE THOUGHT STOPPING

- Performers can suffer from negative self talk, using phrases such as 'I am not going to win this', or 'my opponent is better than me'.
- Converting to more positive thinking & self talk will reduce negativity & provide more optimistic/focussed attitude.

POSITIVE THINKING / SELF TALK

- Using positive set phrases repeatedly can help reduce stress & anxiety, as the performer is able to focus the attention on performance instead of any negative thoughts they may have.
- Can also contribute to maintaining relevant arousal levels.

MINDFULNESS

- Concentrating on the 'present' & it is quite often used in conjunction with meditation.
- Allows the performer to relax, reduce stress & anxiety & focus on the current task, not something in the future.
- eg a batter in cricket may be worried about getting into position for an inswinger (bowl) rather than playing each ball on its merits.

RATIONAL THINKING

- The way performers perceive certain situations is crucial to how they respond to certain stressors.
- In pressurised situations, performers can make (usual) decisions based on their perception eg if they fear a situation due to the risk of injury, irrational decisions are likely to be made.
- Performers should be reassured during these situations
- Training sessions planned to cater for a variety of scenarios to prepare for 'real-life' experiences.
- Should ensure more rational thinking on a regular basis.

SOMATIC STRESS MANAGEMENT TECHNIQUES

PRE-GAME ROUTINES

- Many coaches have a set routine for players/performers prior to the game.

- This may include some individual time, but the warm up through to the game generally follows the same pattern & it is used in part to get players focused & therefore reduce anxiety before a performance.

- Pre-game routines could be as simple as timings & type of food eaten, to superstitions.
  - eg underwear worn, or a 'ritual'
  - eg Pacific Island nations performing a Haka before a contest.

BIOFEEDBACK

- The use of physiological measuring equipment (i.e heart rate monitors, blood pressure data etc), so performers are aware of how their body responds to certain situations.

- Allows performers to understand their body more, to aid controlling their anxiety & stress levels.

REMEMBER...

- COGNITIVE (psychological), focusses on the mind.

- SOMATIC (physiological), focusses on the body.

CENTERING TECHNIQUE

- Assists performers on how to focus on a strong point (the spot) in the body & to imagine being in that 'perfect state' (the centre).

- Redirecting energy to the centre of the body through centring techniques such as imagery, use of cues & controlled breathing, maintaining a sense of calm.

- Aim - reduce anxiety and stress.

PROGRESSIVE MUSCULAR RELAXATION (PMR)

- The use of PMR is said to reduce muscle tension, improve sleep patterns & aid quicker overall recovery.

- It involves contraction & relaxation of muscles, usually working from one end of the body to the other.

- The contraction phase helps the performer feel the tension, whilst the relaxation phase assists in 'letting go' the tension.

- A hard technique to master & plenty of practice is required.

BREATHING CONTROL

- Reducing breathing rate by taking slower/longer breaths can not only assist in controlling heart rate, but reduce arousal levels & muscle tension.

- Deep inhalations allow for greater O₂ consumption & long controlled exhalations help disperse CO₂ as well as assisting the performer to focus on the task in hand.

3.2.3: Sport psychology

1. **Compare** the interactionalist perspective of learning to the trait theory of personality. (6 marks)

2. **Outline** the three components of attitude within the Wood's Triadic Model. (3 marks)

3. **Evaluate** the Drive Theory of arousal and its application with regards to achieving optimal sporting performance. (8 marks)

4. During a netball match, some players can become over-aroused and/or show signs of anxiety.

   With reference to the 'catastrophe theory', **describe** how over-arousal and anxiety can affect a player's performance. (4 marks)

5. Using examples, **describe** the difference between cognitive and somatic anxiety. (6 marks)

6. Rugby Union is a collision sport that can lead to aggressive behaviour.

   Use the aggressive-cue hypothesis to **explain** how this might occur. (3 marks)

7. **Compare** the different types of aggression in sport. (8 marks)

8. **Suggest** strategies to reduce aggressive play. (4 marks)

9. **Explain** the difference between intrinsic and extrinsic motivation. (4 marks)

10. **Explain** the two dimensions of Achievement Motivation. (4 marks)

11. **Examine** the effect that home advantage has on the performance of a home team. **(8 marks)**

12. **Identify** strategies to reduce social loafing. **(4 marks)**

13. **Describe** the difference between outcome and performance goals. **(2 marks)**

14. **Explain** how a coach could use Weiner's Attributional model to maintain and/or improve motivation after a loss? **(6 marks)**

15. Bandura suggests there are 4 factors that affect a performer's self-efficacy. Using examples, **explain** the 4 factors. **(8 marks)**

16. **Analyse** the most appropriate leadership style(s) for coaching performers in the cognitive stage of learning. **(8 marks)**

17. **Outline** 3 cognitive stress management techniques that performers can use to reduce the negative effects of anxiety. **(3 marks)**

Total marks   /89

3.2.4 Sport and society and the role of technology in physical activity and sport

What students need to learn			Yes	Nearly	No
3.2.4.1: Concepts of physical activity and sport	The characteristics and functions of key concepts and how they create the base of the sporting development continuum.	Physical Recreation Sport. Physical education. School sport.			
	The similarities and the differences between these key concepts.				
3.2.4.2: Development of elite performers in sport	The factors required to support progression from talent identification to elite performance.				
	The generic roles, purpose and the relationship between organisations in providing support and progression from talent identification through to elite performance.	National Governing Bodies. National Institutes of Sport. UK Sport.			
	The support services provided by National Institutes of Sports for talent development.				

	The key features of UK Sport's World Class Performance Programme, Gold Event Series and Talent Identification and Development.	Or equivalent current named programmes.			
3.2.4.3: Ethics in sport	Understanding of the key terms relating to ethics in sport.	Amateurism, the Olympic Oath, sportsmanship, gamesmanship, win ethic.			
	Positive and negative forms of deviance in relation to the performer.				
3.2.4.4: Violence in sport	The causes and implications of violence in sport.	Performer. Spectator. Sport.			
	Strategies for preventing violence within sport to the performer and spectator.				
3.2.4.5: Drugs in sport	The social and psychological reasons behind elite performers using illegal drugs and doping methods to aid performance.				
	The physiological effects of drugs on the performer and their performance.	Erythropoietin (EPO). Anabolic steroids. Beta blockers.			

	The positive and negative implications to the sport and the performer of drug taking.	Physiological adaptations. Social and psychological rewards (for the sport and the performer). Negative impact on current and future health. Social and psychological repercussions (for the sport and the performer).			
	Strategies for elimination of performance enhancing drugs in sport.				
	Arguments for and against drug taking and testing.	**Testing procedures will not be examined.**			
3.2.4.6: Sport and the law	The uses of sports legislation.	Performers (contracts, injury, loss of earnings). Officials (negligence). Coaches (duty of care). Spectators (safety, hooliganism).			

3.2.4.7: Impact of commercialisation on physical activity and sport and the relationship between sport and the media	The positive and negative impact of commercialisation, sponsorship and the media.	Performer. Coach. Official. Audience. Sport.			
3.2.4.8: The role of technology in physical activity and sport	Understanding of technology for sports analytics.	Use of technology in data collection (quantitative and qualitative, objective and subjective, validity and reliability of data). Video and analysis programmes. Testing and recording equipment (metabolic cart for indirect calorimetry). Use of GPS and motion tracking software and hardware. Maintaining data integrity.			

		Functions of sports analytics.	Monitor fitness for performance.			
			Skill and technique development.			
			Injury prevention.			
			Game analysis.			
			Talent ID/scouting.			
		The development of equipment and facilities in physical activity and sport, and their impact on participation and performance.	Impact of material technology on equipment — adapted (disability, age).			
			Facilities — Olympic legacy, (surfaces, multi-use).			
		The role of technology in sport and its positive and negative impacts.	Sport.			
			Performer.			
			Coach.			
			Audience.			

So what does it look like......

There are 4 stages to this model, starting at the base.

FOUNDATION - in effect
the 'bottom rung', commonly referred to as 'grassroots'.
- Activities are introduced, normally at school at the primary age group.
- Basic skills & movements are introduced and taught eg throwing & catching a ball.
- Some move to participation level.
- Others remain here & do not progress any further.

SPORTING DEVELOPMENT CONTINUUM

- The theory behind this model/structure is that performers **move through the levels/stages as their participation & standard of performance increases & develops.**

PERFORMANCE
- skills develop further by coaching & playing games.
- Standard improves (county/regional level). More structured competition (leagues & cups).

ELITE
- The top tier; professional, national, international standard.
- A lot smaller than foundation level; far fewer performers.
- Some move all the way through to here, though most stay at one of the 3 other stages/levels.

There are 4 levels to learn...

ELITE (highest)
PERFORMANCE
PARTICIPATION
FOUNDATION (lowest)

ELITE
PERFORMANCE
PARTICIPATION
FOUNDATION

PARTICIPATION
- Choice now involved.
- Main aims; to have fun, enjoyment & socialise.
- It is non-compulsory eg teams at the weekend.
- Competitive games & skills develop further.
- Can be 'Vets' still playing for fitness & enjoyment. eg 3rd team.

112

The differences between Physical Recreation, Sport, Physical Education & School Sport.

Physical Recreation	Sport	Physical Education (PE)	School sport
Fun and enjoyable which is often informal.	Sport has more stringent rules, a more regulated, structured and is organised.	Physical Education is the planned learning that takes place in school curriculum timetabled time that follows the national curriculum..	School sport is more intense exercise which requires specific skills.
Voluntary and a choice where full commitment is not always required.	Sport tends to require more time and commitment.	'Learning to move' (becoming more physically competent) and 'moving to learn' (learning through movement, a range of skills and understandings beyond physical activity, such as co-operating with others).	School sport often involves playing competitively against other teams (intra or inter-school fixtures).
Participation Level of the sporting continuum.	More specialist equipment e.g. full cricket kit bag.	Delivered and inclusive to all students.	Goals are performance focussed.
Performers participate due to the health and fitness benefits.	Qualified coaches and officials involved.	Focussed on developing key skills not necessarily game orientated e.g. catching and running.	Performed as part of extra-curricular time.

Retired performers from the elite or performance levels who want to maintain health and fitness standards for healthy living.	Competitive with the aim of winning.	PE tends to be less competitive.	Elitist with a low percentage of school pupils involved.
Used to help people relieve stress and tension.	Highly skilled.	PE classes are compulsory in schools until the age of 16.	Develops skills, techniques and is often an extension of PE in a competitive environment.
Great way to socialise.	Planned tactics and strategies used in competition.	Goals are generally associated with personal development	Organised competitions from NGB's.
Life long involvement.	Regular structured training with high levels of conditioning required.	PE involves children learning and experiencing a range of activities.	Sometimes external coaches involved.

THE FACTORS REQUIRED TO SUPPORT PROGRESSION TO ELITE PERFORMANCE

SOCIAL FACTORS

SUPPORT SYSTEMS
- Family, friends, coaches & mentors play a vital role in emotional and practical support & offering encouragement.

SOCIO-ECONOMIC STATUS
- Financial support is required for memberships & subs are required to join clubs.
- Certain sports (eg skiing) are more expensive than others & can have a big impact on progress.

COACHING QUALITY
- Having access to expert, experienced coaches can help speed up progression (physically & strategically).

NETWORKING
- Quite often, having a bigger network can lead to more opportunities to progress & exposure at higher levels.

PEER INFLUENCE
- The peer group that time is spent with can influence progression as well as the level of the performer's ability. in that peer group, as there needs to be challenge to improve.

GROWTH MINDSET
- An openness to learning, not being afraid to make mistakes, taking feedback, goal setting & continuously improving skills are necessary for continual progress.

PERSONAL FACTORS

INTRINSIC MOTIVATION
- The individual's drive to succeed, willingness to work hard & resilience to overcome setbacks are crucial to progression.

PHYSICAL ATTRIBUTES
- Athletic ability, high levels of fitness, high pain threshold & adaptability are all crucial in becoming an elite performer.

MENTAL/EMOTIONAL ATTRIBUTES
- Mental toughness, commitment, discipline & the capacity to handle pressure are essential personal traits.

THE FACTORS REQUIRED TO SUPPORT PROGRESSION TO ELITE PERFORMANCE II

DISABILITY
- Now much higher profile after London 2012 Olympics.
- Events at Diamond League athletics.
- Barriers still at local/school level.
- Issues... funding, access, coaching, equipment and discrimination.

ETHNICITY
- Religion & culture can influence sports played. eg. cricket.
- Racist abuse still aimed at Black footballers. eg. The Euro 2020.

EQUAL ACCESS
- Having fair access to high quality training, coaching & competitive opportunities regardless of race, gender, socio-economic status or disability is fundamental for identifying & nurturing talent.

LOCATION
- Ability to access facilities/ resources.
- Locality a huge factor! Near a swimming pool or leisure centre? Access transport?
- Near the outdoors? eg. The Lake District.

REPRESENTATION
- Encouraging diversity in talent pools fosters an inclusive environment for all.

POLICIES ON INCLUSION
- Institutional support for equality. eg. anti-discrimination policies & financial support for under represented groups - level up.

CULTURAL AND EQUALITY FACTORS

GENDER
- Most sports now played by both sexes. eg. football, rugby. Netball still has less media coverage.
- #ThisGirlCan campaign launched in 2015 highly successful.
- Activity Rates - Men 65.9%
  - Women 61.2% (regular)
  Active Lives survey 2022/23.
- Why? Traditional roles (homemaker), lack of role models.

AGE
- Age restrictions on some sports. eg. Boxing.
- As you get older, you have more responsibilities (work, children), less 'leisure time.'
- OAPs 'stereotype' of playing golf & bowls. More time, less money. Social aspect of sport very important.
- Children rely on parents for transport & to pay for clubs (links to Socio- Economic - previous page).

NATIONAL GOVERNING BODIES

OLYMPIC SPORTS

... such as rowing (British Rowing), cycling (British Cycling) & badminton (Badminton England) receive a lot/most of their funding through UK Sport every 4 years, based on their performance at the previous Olympic Games.

FUNDING

- NGBs receive money through the following avenues.
  - Sport England funding
  - UK Sport funding
  - Sponsorship
  - TV deals
  - Club affiliation fees.
  - Merchandise & ticket sales.

MEDIA COVERAGE

including TV, radio, newspapers can help drive this through advertising & promotion & the coverage of games. e.g. WSL football matches on BBC & Sky.

Inspiring Positive Change run by the FA for women's/girls football, with the aim to boost numbers playing, volunteering, coaching & international success!

LOBBY FOR FUNDING

PROFESSIONAL SPORTS

... such as football (the FA), rugby union & league (the RFU & RFL) & cricket (the ECB) tend to get most of their funding through TV deals & sponsorship.

NGBs

- Initially established in the latter years of the 1800s by the 'Old Boys' from the Oxbridge Universities (Oxford & Cambridge) to provide sports with a set of codified laws, rules & regulations.

- Initially developed with the view of recreation - amateur sport.

- Were based on a decentralised system, local associations were self governing.

- However most NGBs are based on a centralised model today where rules, initiatives & policies come from a centralised hub. County & local associations apply them.

* More in book 1, page 117.

PROMOTE PARTICIPATION

- NGBs want as many people as possible from as many different user groups to play 'their' sport - EQUAL OPPORTUNITIES.

- Focus on developing the participation pyramid. This increases numbers at 'grassroots' up to 'elite' standard.

- How?

INITIATIVES & POLICIES

- Can be developed to promote & increase participation.

e.g. the ECB run AllStars Cricket (aged 5-8) & Dynamos Cricket (aged 8-11) is an 8 week long programme designed for those new to cricket.

WHOLE SPORT PLANS

- Are the delivery contract between....

- **SPORT ENGLAND**

- & each of the 46 funded **NATIONAL GOVERNING BODIES** for sport (**NGBs**).

- More information on **NGBs** on page 117 & in book 1 page 117.

- Whole Sport Plans set out how Exchequer (Government) & Lottery funding will be spent & what outcomes the public can expect to see for this investment. (Medals at World Championships & Olympic Games for example).

- The 2013-2017 Whole Sport Plans were primarily focussed on the 14-25 year old age group, with at least 60% of funding aimed at this demographic

WHOLE SPORT PLAN

- A proportion of the investment formed a 'reward' & incentive fund where money only goes to **NGBs** who perform exceptionally well.

The funding each **NGB** was awarded in the Feb 2017 funding decision can be seen below....

National Governing Body	Participation*	Talent	National teams	2017/21 award
Tennis	£5,193,292	£3,000,000		£8,193,292
Athletics	£7,299,992			£7,299,992
Golf	£6,230,000	£2,250,000		£8,480,000
Netball	£10,500,000	£3,400,000	£3,000,000	£16,900,000
Rugby Union	£10,000,000	£2,600,000		£12,600,000
Angling	£682,500			£682,500
Basketball	£4,730,000			£4,730,000
Sailing**	£3,219,850	£3,150,000		£6,369,850
Canoeing	£3,850,000			£3,850,000
Judo	£3,750,000	£1,075,000		£4,825,000
Rowing	£4,100,000			£4,100,000
Table Tennis	£6,790,000	£1,500,000		£8,290,000
Orienteering	£805,000			£805,000
Handball	£1,265,000	£150,000		£1,415,000
Snowsport	£850,000	£200,000		£1,050,000
Archery**	£285,712	£650,000		£935,712
Boxing**	£364,734	£1,050,000		£1,414,734
Fencing		£500,000		£500,000
Goalball		£200,000		£200,000
Modern Pentathlon		£600,000		£600,000
Basketball (GB)			£1,000,000	£1,000,000
Squash**	£1,141,250			£1,141,250
Football**	£1,012,000	£4,600,000		£5,612,000
Volleyball**	£421,520			£421,520
Wheelchair basketball**	£300,000			£300,000
TOTAL				**£101,715,850**

Key:

* - where applicable includes funding for core markets (regular participants, inactivity, satellite clubs & mass markets).

** - Short term participation award pending full funding application.

NATIONAL INSTITUTES OF SPORT

There is a network of 7 high performance centres across England, where the UKSI provides elite performers & coaches access to high quality facilities
- training, rehabilitation, sports medicine etc.

NIS
- 25th April 2023, the English Institute of Sport (EIS), became known as the UK Sports Institute.
- The UK Sports Institute is the largest single provides of world class science, medicine, technology & engineering services to Olympic & Paralympic sports in the UK.
- The UKSI has played a vital role in contributing to the success of thousands of performers since its inception in 2002.
- The UKSI works with performance directors and coaches within elite sport to identify where expertise can be utilised.

BATH
- Based at the University of Bath.
- Home to a number of sports, including... Modern Pentathlon, Skeleton, Swimming & Wheelchair Fencing.
- Sailing in the S.W (Weymouth).

HOLME PIERREPONT
- Support for Para-Canoeing & Speed Skating.

LILLESHALL
- Based at the National Sports Centre; home to archery & gymnastics.

LOUGHBOROUGH
- Supports a wide range of sports across East Midlands.

MANCHESTER
- Located at Manchester Institute of Health. Also the Head Office of the UKSI

SHEFFIELD
- Supports performers in Boxing, Diving & Para-Table Tennis.

BISHAM ABBEY
- Home to a wide range of performers including... Rowing, Para-Rowing, Hockey & England Women's Rugby.
- Also home to the Intensive Rehabilitation Unit (UKSI/BOA partnership).

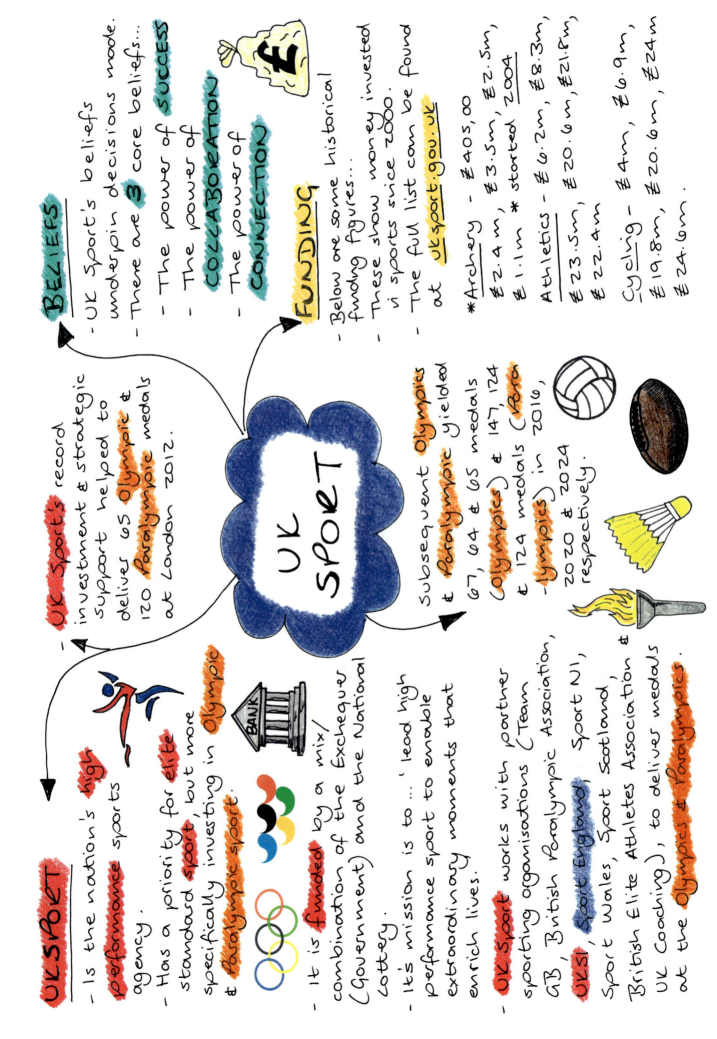

UK SPORT

BELIEFS
- UK Sport's beliefs underpin decisions made.
- There are **3** core beliefs...
  - The power of **SUCCESS**
  - The power of **COLLABORATION**
  - The power of **CONNECTION**

FUNDING
- Below are some historical funding figures...
- These show money invested in sports since 2000.
- The full list can be found at **uksport.gov.uk**

*Archery - £405,00
  £2.4m, £3.5m, £2.5m,
  £1.1m * started 2004

Athletics - £6.2m, £8.3m,
  £23.5m, £20.6m, £21.6m,
  £22.4m

Cycling - £4m, £6.9m,
  £19.8m, £20.6m, £24m
  £24.6m.

UK SPORT

- UK Sport's record investment & strategic support helped to deliver 65 Olympic & 120 Paralympic medals at London 2012.

- Subsequent Olympics & Paralympics yielded 67, 64 & 65 medals (Olympics) & 147, 124 & 124 medals (Paralympics) in 2016, 2020 & 2024 respectively.

UKSPORT
- Is the nation's high performance sports agency.
- Has a priority for elite standard sport, but more specifically investing in Olympic & Paralympic sport.
- It is funded by a mix/combination of the Exchequer (Government) and the National Lottery.
- It's mission is to ... 'lead high performance sport to enable extraordinary moments that enrich lives.'
- UK Sport works with partner sporting organisations (Team GB, British Paralympic Association, UKSI, Sport England, Sport NI, Sport Wales, Sport Scotland, British Elite Athletes Association & UK Coaching), to deliver medals at the Olympics & Paralympics.

INJURY PREVENTION & REHABILITATION

- Access to rehabilitation experts who work on injury prevention strategies & facilitate recovery from injuries to ensure performers can return to peak performance quickly.

NUTRITION SUPPORT

- Nutritionalists work to develop a personalised diet plan to support training regimes, recovery & competition to optimise fuel consumption for performance.

PSYCHOLOGICAL SUPPORT

- Sport Psychologists help with ways to overcome the emotional rigours & coping strategies for elite level sport.

SUPPORT PROVIDED BY NIS

- In the UK, National Institutes of Sport (NIS), UK Sport & NGBs work closely to identify, support & develop talent. Here are the key services...

TALENT ID

- & development. NIS, work with NGBs to identify talented individuals across different sports. eg UK Sport's Talent ID initiative

SPECIALISED COACHING

- Is provided to performers on talent pathways to ensure they receive training that aligns with their development stage.

SPORTS SCIENCE SUPPORT

- Performance analysis, biomechanics support to improve technique & to reduce the chance of further injuries and strength & conditioning (S&C), to further improve capabilities.

ACCESS TO HIGH PERFORMANCE FACILITIES

- Access to world class facilities at one of the National Institutes of Sport.

ATHLETE LIFESTYLE PROGRAMMES

- Ways to manage lives outside of sport at the elite level, from being able to cope with pressure, to preparing for competition.

FINANCIAL SUPPORT

- & grants. Performers can access funding eg World Class Programme.

TALENT IDENTIFICATION

UK SPORT
- They analyse the applications/people are invited to start the phase process outlined below...

PHASE ONE
- A range of generic physical & skill based tests (carried out at various testing centres around the UK).
- Tests include... sprints, jumps, aerobic fitness & upper/lower body strength tests.
- Specific tests will depend on the sport.
- Selection process also includes an in depth analysis of each athlete's training & competition history.

CONFIRMATION PHASE
- Athletes selected need to commit to 6-12 months confirmation phase.
- Immersed into the sports training environment.
- Rates of progress are tracked to further assess suitability.
- Unsuccessful athletes move towards club system.

UK SPORT TALENT ID MODEL
- Multiple phases when looking for talent.
- Campaigns start with a local talent search either with the general public or with the sports communities involving athletes submitting an application form to UK Sport.

AND DEVELOPMENT IN THE UK
- The GB team & UK Sport went through hard times in the 1990's, but an announcement on the 1st March 1999 by the Government expanding the UK Sports Institutes (UKSI) provision, with a view to concentrating on Olympic sports & those minority sports lacking a commercial element.
- Similar to the Australian model, the UKSI is supported by a network of centres across

England...
- Bath.
- Holme Pierrepont.
- Lilleshall.
- Loughborough.
- Manchester (Head office of UKSI).
- Sheffield.
- Bisham Abbey.

Home nations also have national centres in...
- Scotland
- Wales
- Northern Ireland.

PHASE TWO & THREE
- Are designed to further assess an athlete's suitability for a sport & better equip them for the journey ahead.
- The pathway from identification to world class performance is outlined.
- Sessions may include... functional movement screening, medical screening, performance lifestyle workshops & psychology and behavioural assessments.

TALENT ID INITIATIVES

WORLD CLASS PROGRAMME
- Funded & run by **UK Sport** (the elite sports agency in the UK).

WORLD CLASS PODIUM
- Designed to support sports & athletes with medal capabilities (realistic) at **Olympic Games** or gold medal capabilities (realistic) at **Paralympic Games**.
- Are a maximum of 4 years away from the podium.

WORLD CLASS PODIUM POTENTIAL
- Designed to support the stage of the pathway immediately below Podium.
- Supports sports & athletes that have demonstrated realistic medal winning capabilities for future **Olympic or Paralympic Games**.
- Typically 4-6 years away from podium.

PERFORMANCE FOUNDATIONS
- Home Nations talent pathways where highly talented athletes are first identified, confirmed & prepared to meet the increased demands of the **WORLD class** environment.
- Athletes at PF level have the potential to graduate to **PP** within 1-4 years.

List (top of pathway to bottom):
- PODIUM
- PODIUM POTENTIAL
- PERFORMANCE FOUNDATIONS
- NATIONAL AGE GROUP PROGS
- REGIONAL PROGRAMMES
- COUNTY PROGRAMMES
- COMMUNITY, SCHOOL ETC

CURRENTLY
- **UK Sport** & the **UKSI** work together with **Team GB** & **Paralympics GB** in search of athletes of the future called

FROM HOME 2 THE GAMES
- The initiative has been designed to discover untapped potential from all communities in the UK.
- More specifically 11-23 year olds who are physically active to participate in an **Olympic sport** & 15-34 year olds with an impairment that makes them eligible in a **Paralympic sport**.
- Different initiatives are conducted at different points, but specific egs include:

Bounce4Gold   **Power 2 Paris**

- Canoeing... aimed at 15-17 year olds who compete at regional level & 18-25 year olds competing at national standard (in any sport) who believe that can achieve **Olympic** success.
- Performance Pathways Team now work with other **NGBs**

GIRLS FOR GOLD
- The single most extensive female talent recruitment drive ever undertaken in Great Britain, seeking to find motivated females with (Para) **Olympic** ambition.
- **UK Sport** worked with **UKSI** & GB Canoeing, launching the first in a series of **Girls4Gold** campaigns.

GOLD EVENT SERIES

- This forms part of the plans to develop **Government support** for hosting major **international sporting events** & continue the momentum generated by London 2012 (Olympics) & Glasgow 2014 (Commonwealth Games).

- It has just been agreed for Glasgow to host a 'scaled down' version of the Games in 2026 after The Australian state of Victoria withdrew due to rising costs.

- This plan focusses on attracting **big sporting events**, like World Championships, European Championships & other specific major sporting events.
- The events are targeted to support

- British athletes preparation and qualification for the **Olympic and Paralympic Games**.

- It also provides an opportunity for 2.5 million spectators to continue to experience world class **Olympic and Paralympic sports** on home soil.

- The **National Lottery funded £27 million Gold Event Series** will aim to bring over 70 of the world's most prestigious sporting events to the UK, including 36 World and European Championships. eg: Gymnastics, Hockey, Rugby League, Triathlon & Eventing.

- The **Gold Event Series** hopes to **generate around £287 million** additional expenditure in host cities and regions across the UK & over 250,000 overseas visitors.

124

WORLD CLASS TALENT TRANSFER PROGRAMMES

TALENT TRANSFER PROGRAMME

- The UKSI & UK Sport have worked together to recruit performers onto what is known as the

TALENT TRANSFER PROGRAMME, or as it is sometimes called, the talent 'swap shop.'

- The programme aims to recruit performers that have already retired, or nearing retirement & provide them with a 'second chance' opportunity to switch sports & contribute to the success of Team GB (in the lead up to 2012).

- It was introduced with the belief that many performers that didn't quite make it as an 'elite athlete' may have skills

that are transferrable, eg, physiological, technical, perceptual, motor and conceptual & required to succeed in a different, alternative sport.

- An example of someone who has transferred using this programme is Shelly Rudman. She moved from the 400m hurdles to Bob skeleton & won Silver at the 2006 Winter Olympics.

- There are also some instances where retired gymnasts have also transferred into the diving team.

- This makes sense as there are many transferrable skills between the 2 disciplines/ activities.

TALENT HEALTH CHECK

- Health checks are used to confirm & develop practices with regards talent identification.

- Allows UK Sport to gauge an understanding of current prospects for informed decisions in the next Olympic cycle.

- Findings help shape UK Sport Talent strategy. (Latest Post Paris 24... 'Find Your Greatness.')

THE MODERN OLYMPIC GAMES

THE OLYMPIC OATH

'In the name of the athletes, we promise to take part in these Olympic Games, respecting & abiding by the rules & in the spirit of fair play. We all commit ourselves to sport without doping & cheating. We do this for the glory of sport, for the honour of our teams & in respect for the Fundamental Principles of Olympism.'

Pierre de Coubertin

FIRST GAMES
- 896 in Athens.
- 9 sports, 3
- 5 days, 32 events.
- 311 athletes ... but no women! That was in Paris in 1900.

- This is one of the reasons why countries (specifically cities) bid to host major sporting events like the Olympics (& World Cups, Commonwealth Games etc).

- It is a way to support local communities with the development of better infrastructure, as well as massive financial gain (spectators, tourism).

- However, there are issues.

PIERRE DE COUBERTIN

- Baron Pierre de Coubertin can be credited as the 'founder' of the modern day Olympic movement.

- He developed the ideals surrounding the modern Olympic Games, with the idea of Olympism becoming clear in the Olympic Charter as...

'... a philosophy of life, exalting & combining in a balanced whole the qualities of body, will and mind. Blending sport with culture and education, Olympism seeks to create a way of life based on the joy of effort, the educational value of good example, social responsibility and respect for universal fundamental ethical principles.'

De Coubertin wanted to 'revive' the Ancient Olympic Games 'ideal' & inspired by the Much Wenlock Games in Shropshire, set about doing so... (AQA Book 1 P.109).

AIM OF OLYMPISM

- Is to demonstrate how sport can help foster better relationships between communities & nations, helping us to live in harmony with one another.

OLYMPIC VALUES

- EXCELLENCE
- FRIENDSHIP
- RESPECT

AMATEURS AND PROFESSIONALS

ROOTS
- ... dates back to Roman times, where Gladiators were paid sportsmen!
- Relatively short careers, so look to maximise earning potential with sponsorship deals.
- eg - Lionel Messi & Adidas, Cristiano Ronaldo & Nike.

PROFESSIONALISM
- Lucrative contracts now on offer to performers.
- One moment that changed the global stage was the inclusion of the 'Dream Team' at the Barcelona Olympics in 1992.
- The team made up of NBA superstars represented the USA as the first fully professional team in the Olympics.

- Players such as Michael Jordan, Magic Johnson & Larry Bird played in the most anticipated event at the Games.
- Popularity in the sport skyrocketed & had a knock on effect for professional sport in general.

- At the start of the '91-92' season, there were 23 international players from 18 countries on NBA rosters.
- By '23-24', this had increased to 125 players from 40 countries!

PROFESSIONALS
- Paid.
- Play sport for their job/profession.
- Play for financial gain (extrinsic reward)

AMATEURS
- Unpaid.
- Play sport for the 'love of the game.'
- Original idea ... to reflect the spirit of the Ancient Olympics, that fair play, team spirit & participation are of a far higher value than material reward.

- As commercialisation & sponsorship have increased, more & more traditionally 'amateur' sports have now, in effect become professional eg. athletics.

SPORTSMANSHIP AND GAMESMANSHIP

COMMERCIALISM

- The increase in commercialism has had many positive effects on sport.
- ... however due to increased pressure on performance & a 'win at all costs' attitude at the elite level, the rise in issues surrounding gamesmanship has increased.
- Players vie for bigger deals (both in terms of contracts with their team and sponsorship deals).
- The pressure to secure their legacy & future prospects can come down to a single game or event.
- At times there is not always a clear line between gamesmanship & deviant behaviours (eg diving/simulation in football).
- This is one of the reasons why the increase in technology on the court/pitch has helped to eradicate certain behaviours. (eg off the ball incidents in football that may be missed by the referee).
- Such technology includes... replays, pitch side microphones & numerous camera angles.

ETIQUETTE

- Is the way sportsmen/women behave whilst playing (in a positive manner). Very similar to sportsmanship. Promotes fairplay.

SPORTSMANSHIP

- 'Play & abide by the rules', win & lose graciously.
- Sportsmen & women are role models & should adhere to the written (& unwritten) rules of the sport.
- Fair play, respect & polite behaviours are all important.
  eg shaking hands at the end of the game.
  Helping an injured opponent.
  Being respectful to officials.

CONTRACT TO COMPETE

- agreeing to play by the rules, trying to win, but also allowing your opponent to play.
- Want to win, but not at all costs!
- Links with etiquette & sportsmanship.

GAMESMANSHIP

- 'The use of dubious though not illegal methods to win or gain an advantage'. 'Bending' the rules not breaking them!
- All done with the intention of winning!
  eg timewasting in football, sledging in cricket to get a psychological advantage.
- diving in football after a tackle to influence the ref to give a free kick ... or is it DEVIANCE!?

THE WIN ETHIC

- This is often referred to (as has already been mentioned) as a 'win at all costs' attitude

- It has increasingly become 'the norm' in professional sport & has even filtered down into the amateur ranks.

- The win ethic is usually associated with VINCE LOMBARDI, who is best known for coaching the Green Bay Packers to 5 championships in 7 years (NFL). The 'LOMBARDIAN ETHIC' was created.

- He has been quoted as saying ... 'winning isn't everything, it is the only thing' and 'if it doesn't matter who wins or loses, then why do they keep score?'

EXAMPLES

- Baseball's biggest co-ordinated scandal occurred in 2017, with the Houston Astros 'stealing signs' (hand instructions) using ball park cameras & communicating them

using bangs of rubbish bin lids.

- The team did this during the 2017 & 2018 seasons, including the 2017 play offs & their World Series win over the LA Dodgers.

- In 2018, some of the Australian cricket team were caught (on TV) using sandpaper to scuff up the cricket ball to improve it's ability to reverse swing. This can be hard to defend as a batting team and this was used to try & gain an advantage in the game.

- The win ethic can be seen in many aspects of sport in the 21st century...
- Positive & negative media posts for winning & losing.

WIN ETHIC

- Deviance in sport. eg - PEDs, drugs, violence, illegal bets etc.

- High turnover of underperforming coaches & staff (& performers).

- Emphasis on a winner. eg - golden point in Rugby League.

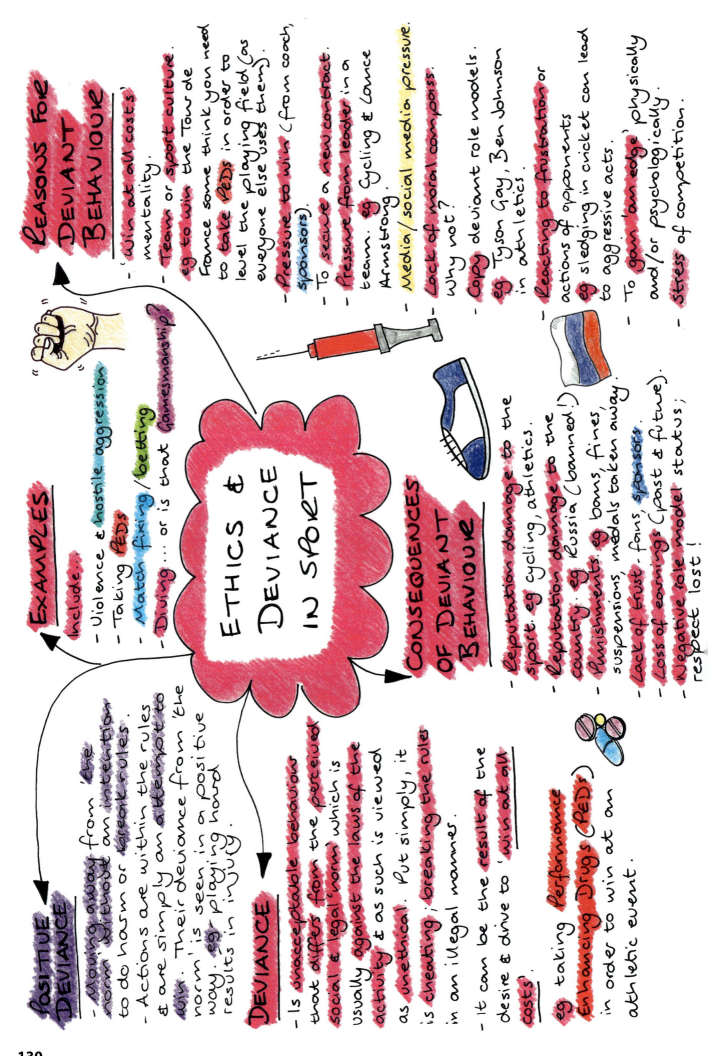

Reasons For Deviant Behaviour

- 'Win at all costs' mentality.
- Team or sport culture. eg to win the Tour de France some think you need to take PEDs in order to level the playing field (as everyone else uses them).
- Pressure to win (from coach, sponsors).
- To secure a new contract.
- Pressure from leader in a team. eg Cycling & Lance Armstrong.
- Media / social media pressure.
- Lack of moral compass. Why not?
- Copy deviant role models. eg Tyson Gay, Ben Johnson in athletics.
- Reacting to frustration or actions of opponents eg sledging in cricket can lead to aggressive acts.
- To gain 'an edge' physically and/or psychologically.
- Stress of competition.

Examples

Include...
- Violence & hostile aggression
- Taking PEDs
- Match fixing / betting
- Diving... or is that Gamesmanship?

Ethics & Deviance in Sport

Positive Deviance

- Moving away from 'the norm' without an intention to do harm or break rules.
- Actions are within the rules & are simply an attempt to win. Their deviance from the norm is seen in a positive way. eg playing hard results in injury.

Deviance

- Is unacceptable behaviour that differs from the perceived social & legal 'norm', which is usually against the laws of the activity & as such is viewed as unethical. Put simply, it is cheating; breaking the rules in an illegal manner.
- It can be the result of the desire & drive to 'win at all costs'.

eg taking Performance Enhancing Drugs (PEDs) in order to win at an athletic event.

Consequences of Deviant Behaviour

- Reputation damage to the sport. eg cycling, athletics.
- Reputation damage to the country. eg Russia (banned!)
- Punishments. eg bans, fines, suspensions, medals taken away.
- Lack of trust. fans, sponsors.
- Loss of earnings (past & future).
- Negative role model status; respect lost!

SPORT AND DEVIANCE

MATCH FIXING

- Occurs when a game or match is influenced (generally for financial gain).
- eg in the London 2012 Olympic Games, the Chinese, Indonesian & South Korean badminton teams were found to be losing deliberately in order to face potentially 'easier' teams in the latter stages. All teams were disqualified & charged with abusing & demeaning the sport of badminton.

A BUNG

- Is an unauthorised & undisclosed payment to a person (in a high position) at a club.
- Agents attempting to get the best deal for their player may pay the manager a bung.

SIMULATION

- ... or diving!
- Is an unsportsmanlike act whereby a player tries to gain an unfair advantage by pretending to have been fouled & falling to the ground, with the aim of influencing the referee to give a foul, waste time, or get the opposition player booked.
- In 2017/18 the FA updated the rule on simulation & diving & have stated it must be sanctioned as unsporting behaviour (misconduct, punishable by a yellow card).
- Instances of simulation can also now be looked at retrospectively, if missed by the referee.

BETTING SYNDICATES

- Are a type of pool betting, involving two or more people that predict results of sporting events & provide odds for gamblers.
- eg in 2010, young Pakistani fast bowler Mohammed Amir was found guilty of bowling deliberate illegal deliveries (no balls) in a test series v England, in order to fall in with bets placed by syndicates. This got Amir banned from Pakistani Cricket for 5 years, alongside fellow pace bowler Mohammed Asif & captain Salmon Butt for the same length of time by the ICC.

BRIBERY

- A bribe is where someone takes/receives something with the intention of influencing the outcome.
- eg Sepp Blatter (former FIFA president) was found to have accepted undue economic benefits (£18 million or so) for various conflicts of interest in relation to awarding various tournaments to various countries dating back to 2011.
- This included the World Cups to Russia (2018) & Qatar (2022).
- Blatter was banned from any involvement in football for 6 years (from 2015). In 2021 he was given another 6 years & 8 months suspension.

STRATEGIES TO PREVENT VIOLENCE WITHIN SPORT TO THE PERFORMER

PUNISHING PLAYERS

- For foul play/offences eg yellow/red cards, fines, suspensions.

CITING PLAYERS

- Applying the above after a post match review.

LOSING SPONSORS

- If a performer repeatedly/seriously performs violent acts.

DISMISSED FROM TEAM

- Suspended from the team or contract terminated.

MORE OFFICIALS

- To spot 'foul play'. eg TMO in rugby, VAR in football & 3 on court officials in basketball.

VIOLENCE IN SPORT

COACHES & PERFORMERS

- Believe that a certain amount of aggression is required to achieve success in sport.
- This can be difficult at times, depending on the sport, situation & the individual to find the correct level needed for optimal success.
- Sometimes the word aggression is used interchangeably with assertion. This is the more appropriate term for coaches & performers to use to embed into a performer's behaviour.
- Behaviours relate to proactive, firm and decisive play.

- There is no intention to harm an opponent.
- The performer uses all permitted means to achieve the set goal, all basic features of assertive play.

EDUCATION

- Programmes linked to fair play.

POINT DEDUCTION

- Affects the whole team.

ROLE MODELS

- Promoted by media who engage in fair play.

COUNSELLING

- For violent performers.

132

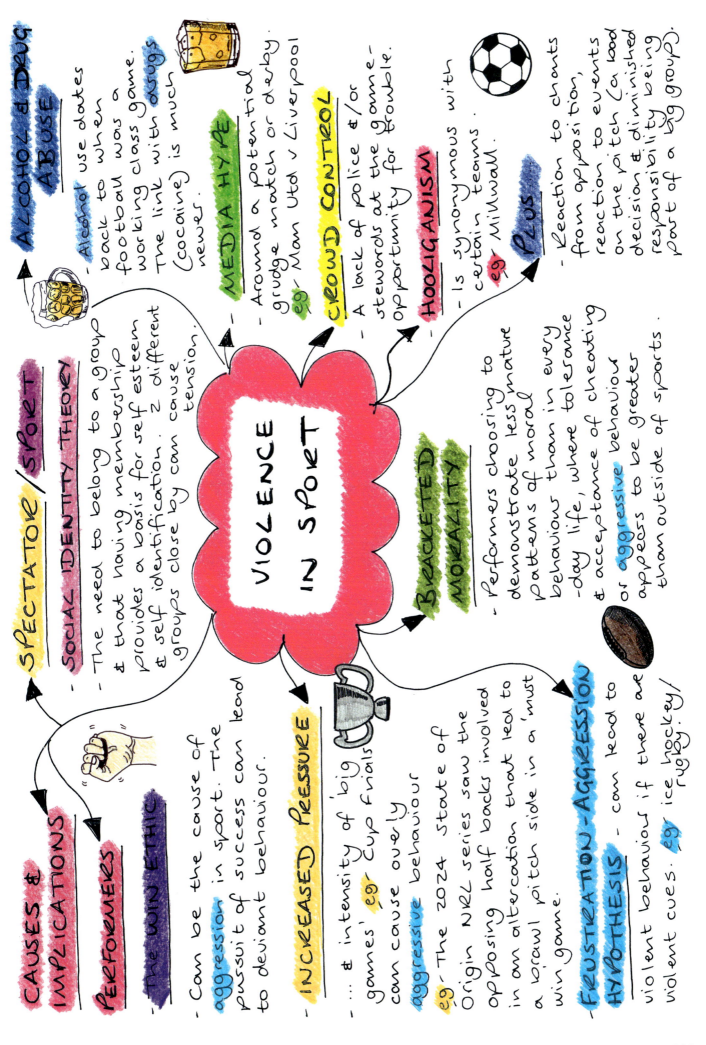

VIOLENCE IN SPORT

ALCOHOL & DRUG ABUSE
- Alcohol use dates back to when football was a working class game. The link with drugs (cocaine) is much newer.

MEDIA HYPE
- Around a potential grudge match or derby. eg. Man Utd v Liverpool

CROWD CONTROL
- A lack of police &/or stewards at the game. opportunity for trouble.

HOOLIGANISM
- Is synonymous with certain teams. eg. Millwall.

PIUS
- Reaction to chants from opposition, reaction to events on the pitch (a bad decision & diminished responsibility being part of a big group).

SPECTATOR/SPORT

SOCIAL IDENTITY THEORY
- The need to belong to a group & that having membership provides a basis for self esteem & self identification. 2 different groups close by can cause tension.

CAUSES & IMPLICATIONS

PERFORMERS

The WIN ETHIC
- Can be the cause of aggression in sport. The pursuit of success can lead to deviant behaviour.

INCREASED PRESSURE
- ... & intensity of big games' eg. Cup Finals can cause overly aggressive behaviour.
- eg. The 2024 State of Origin NRL series saw the opposing half backs involved in an altercation that lead to a brawl pitch side in a 'must win game.

BRACKETED MORALITY
- Performers choosing to demonstrate less mature patterns of moral behaviour than in every-day life, where tolerance & acceptance of cheating or aggressive behaviour or aggress to be greater than outside of sports.

FRUSTRATION-AGGRESSION HYPOTHESIS
- can lead to violent behaviour if there are violent cues. eg. ice hockey/ rugby.

COMBATTING DEVIANT BEHAVIOUR

SUPPORTERS / FANS
- ... can create a great atmosphere eg European Cup matches under the 'lights' & give home team an advantage.
- However, as can be seen there is a potential for costly, negative effects.

INCREASED TICKET PRICES
- This may deter some would be troublemakers from attending games/matches due to the prohibitive cost.

SEGREGATION OF FANS
- keep opposing fans apart. Gap with stewards/police. (Again costly).

FAMILY FRIENDLY
- as a result less instances of violence.

EDUCATIONAL CAMPAIGNS
- Players/role models used. eg 'Kick it Out'.

IMPROVED SECURITY
- checks at turnstiles, CCTV inside & out, more police, better trained stewards, police spotters. (Costly).

GOOD
spectator behaviour or etiquette means watching & behaving in a respectful manner.

eg not booing the opposing national anthem, being quiet during rallies in tennis, place kicks in rugby & tee shots in golf.

SUPPORTERS
- Legal action against supporters does occur, with some forms of unacceptable behaviour becoming more commonplace (eg attacking players, officials, running onto the pitch).
- Spectators must act within the law when at a game.
- They are not permitted to enter the field of play or use racist/homophobic language, something most NGB's are trying to eradicate with the help of 'Kick it Out'.
- Clubs & sports governing bodies employ a number of strategies focussed on spectator behaviour, including:

ALCOHOL RESTRICTIONS & EARLY KICK OFFS
- Games start before the pubs open. Limit sales, banned in the away end (though this may cause trouble?). Not allowed in view of the pitch (football).

TRAVEL RESTRICTIONS & BANNING ORDERS
- stop known hooligans attending games. Attend police station on match day. Bans, fines... even prison!

DRUGS IN SPORT

WINNING MENTALITY

- The pressure to meet their own high expectations can lead performers to seek an easier option & use PEDs.

FEAR OF FAILURE

- The fear of not performing at their best, losing or not meeting the standards of everyone involved (fans, coaches etc), can lead to PED use.

MANAGING MENTAL HEALTH

- Some performers turn to drugs to boost confidence & manage mental strain due to the pressure of elite sport.

PSYCHOLOGICAL REASONS

COPING WITH PRESSURE

- The constant pressure to perform at the elite level can create anxiety, pushing performers to use substances to give them an edge!

THE SOCIAL AND PSYCHOLOGICAL REASONS BEHIND ELITE PERFORMERS USING ILLEGAL DRUGS & DOPING METHODS

- Elite performers face heightened pressure to succeed, to maintain their status & meet expectations from...
  - themselves
  - their coach
  - the public
  - & the media.

- These pressures, combined with intense competition & financial rewards make some performers turn to Performance Enhancing Drugs (PEDs) to cope with these pressures & to continue excelling at the highest level.

FASTER RECOVERY

- The need to recover quickly from injuries & return to competition fuels the psychological need to stay relevant, leading some to use PEDs for faster recovery.

DRUGS IN SPORT II

FINANCIAL BENEFITS

- Winning often brings prize money, sponsorships & endorsements. The prospect of losing these can motivate performers to seek illegal performance boosts.

SPONSORSHIP AND FAME

- Performers may feel the pressure to continually perform at the highest level, fearing loss of endorsements if not at their peak.

SOCIAL REASONS

CULTURAL ACCEPTANCE IN SPORT

- Drug use is seen as part of the culture, where performers believe that everyone else are using PEDs, creating a sense of justification for personal use. 'Everyone is doing it ... I'm not being left behind!'

- Some performers may face pressure from coaches, team mates or sports organisations that subtly (or even overtly!) encourage the use of PEDs to enhance team success or reputation.

CONSTANT SCRUTINY IN THE MEDIA

- The intense focus on performance (& winning!) can lead to heightened expectations, making performers feel like they must live up to unrealistic standards.

INJURY AND AGE

- Injuries and/or the natural decline in performance with age can push performers to use substances that help with faster recovery or prolong their career.

THE PHYSIOLOGICAL EFFECTS OF DRUGS ON THE PERFORMER & THEIR PERFORMANCE

ANABOLIC STEROIDS

- Promotes muscle growth, increases strength & power & improves recovery time (after training/competition).

Benefits - Bodybuilders, weightlifters, & strength focussed sports like rugby & football.

Side Effects - Liver damage, heart disease, high blood pressure, hormonal imbalances, aggression & mood swings.

Males - can cause infertility & breast development.

Females - deepened voice & facial hair growth.

DRUGS IN SPORT III

ERYTHROPOIETIN

- Also known as EPO.
- Naturally occuring in the body.
- Increases red blood cell production, improving O2 delivery to (working) muscles, enhancing endurance.

Benefits - endurance athletes such as cyclists, long distance runners & cross country skiers.

Side Effects - Thicker, more viscous blood, leading to an increased risk of blood clots, heart attacks, stroke, high blood pressure (hypertension) & potentially fatal cardiovascular issues.

BETA BLOCKERS

- Reduces heart rate, muscle tension & blood pressure
- Aids fine motor control & precise movements
- Reduces anxiety & steady's nerves & enhances focus

Benefits - Performers in sports requiring steadiness, such as archery, golf & shooting.

Side Effects - Fatigue, dizziness, depression, low blood pressure & difficulty breathing, especially during high-intensity exercise.

137

SPORT AND DEVIANCE

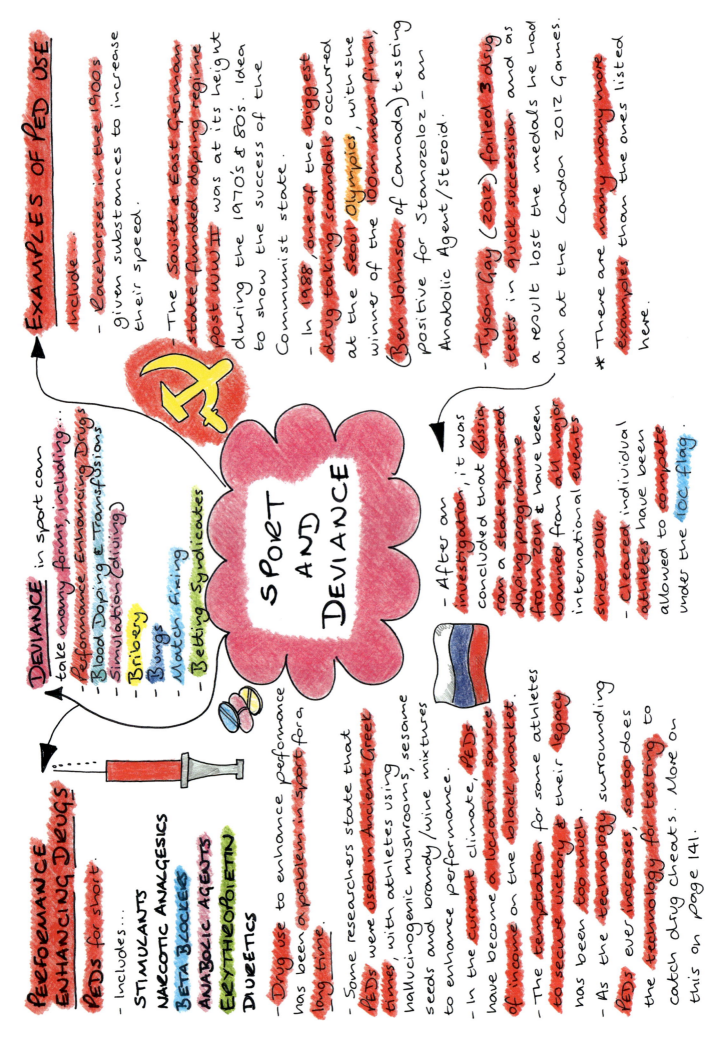

EXAMPLES OF PED USE

Include...

- Racehorses in the 1900s given substances to increase their speed.

- The Soviet & East German state funded doping regime post WWII was at its height during the 1970's & 80's. Idea to show the success of the Communist state.

- In 1988, one of the biggest drug taking scandals occurred at the Seoul Olympics, with the winner of the 100m mens final, (Ben Johnson of Canada) testing positive for Stanozoloz - an Anabolic Agent/Steroid.

- Tyson Gay (2012) failed 3 drug tests in quick succession and as a result lost the medals he had won at the London 2012 Games.

* There are many many more examples than the ones listed here.

- After an investigation, it was concluded that Russia ran a state sponsored doping programme from 2011 & have been banned from all major international events since 2016.

- Cleared individual athletes have been allowed to compete under the IOC flag.

PERFORMANCE ENHANCING DRUGS

PEDs for short.

- Includes...

STIMULANTS
NARCOTIC ANALGESICS
BETA BLOCKERS
ANABOLIC AGENTS
ERYTHEOPOIETIN
DIURETICS

- Drug use to enhance performance has been a problem in sport for a long time.

- Some researchers state that PEDs were used in Ancient Greek times, with athletes using hallucinogenic mushrooms, sesame seeds and brandy/wine mixtures to enhance performance.

- In the current climate, PEDs have become a lucrative source of income on the black market.

- The temptation for some athletes to secure victory & their legacy has been too much.

- As the technology surrounding PEDs ever increases, so too does the technology for testing to catch drug cheats. More on this on page 141.

DEVIANCE in sport can take many forms, including...

- Performance Enhancing Drugs
- Blood Doping & Transfusions
- Simulation (diving)
- Bribery
- Bungs
- Match Fixing
- Betting Syndicates

138

THE POSITIVE & NEGATIVE IMPLICATIONS OF DRUG TAKING

SOCIAL AND PSYCHOLOGICAL REPERCUSSIONS

Loss of Trust and Integrity
- If drug use becomes widespread in a sport & performers are caught doping, it can erode the trust the public have in the sport & performers eg: cycling.

DECLINE IN PARTICIPATION AND PUBLICITY
- Increased doping scandals may discourage the public & younger performers from taking part in that particular sport, which could lead to a decline in sponsorship & media coverage.

PSYCHOLOGICAL
- Performers may feel guilt or emotional stress from drug taking, especially if they feel it is morally wrong.

PSYCHOLOGICAL SATISFACTION
- Due to improvements in performance as a result of taking PEDs, performers may feel a sense of achievement, since they have achieved their goals & potentially won more games/competitions

SOCIAL AND PSYCHOLOGICAL REWARDS

INCREASED POPULARITY
- Due to increased potential in the level of performance, there can be an increase in media coverage, sponsorship & the ability to attract large crowds, which will have a benefit on both the sport and the performer(s).

- This can increase the fame, status, recognition of a performer in society.

SOCIAL MOBILITY
- Performers who come from less priviledged backgrounds may be tempted to use PEDs for the chance of increasing fame, fortune & success and to improve their social standing.

LOSS OF REPUTATION AND SUPPORT
- Performers often face a backlash from fans & sponsors if caught doping, which can have a negative effect on their future involvement (bans & suspension that lead to a loss of career earnings).

NOT ME

THEIR FAULT

STRATEGIES FOR THE ELIMINATION OF PEDS

- The **WORLD ANTI-DOPING AGENCY (WADA)**. More on page 141.

- The **COUNCIL OF EUROPE**.

- The **INTERNATIONAL ANTI-DOPING ARRANGEMENT (IADA)**.

- The **INSTITUTE OF NATIONAL ANTI-DOPING ORGANISATIONS (INADO)**

PROHIBITED SUBSTANCES

- UKAD promotes the prohibited substances & methods list co-ordinated by ~~WADA~~ to performers.
- This list is updated each year on January 1st.

- UKAD works as an active participant in the fight against doping on a global scale & focusses on an international approach, working with...

UKAD

- Stands for UK ANTI-DOPING.

- They are responsible for ensuring that sports bodies in the UK are compliant with the **WORLD ANTI-DOPING CODE**, through implementation and management of the UK's National Anti Doping Policy.

- UKAD was created in December 2009 & their functions include...

  - A prevention through education programme. (eg 100% me).

  - Intelligence led athlete testing across 40+ **Olympic, Paralympic** & professional sports.

  - Investigations and results management authority for the determination of **Anti-Doping Rule Violations (ADRVs)**.

HUNT DOWN

The drug cheats. Test...

HAIR
URINE
NAILS
TEST BLOOD

DRUG TESTING

- First occurred in 1966 European Athletic Championships in Budapest, then 2 years later at the 1968 Olympics in Mexico City.

- A sample tests positive, test B sample. B sample positive = BAN! 1st offence = 4 years.

BIOLOGICAL PASSPORT

- Since 2009, WADA first approved its use, it has been an effective deterrent & way of catching drug cheats.

- Anti-doping organisations have integrated the Biological Passport into their programme to reveal the effects of doping rather than the method or substance used.

- The first version profiled an Athlete's haematological variables (for the detection of blood doping). In 2014 the Steroidal Module was launched to complement this, focussing on an athlete's steroidal variables in urine samples.

- ... however this new data has given athletes insights into doping techniques. Further advanced techniques have been developed regards 'microdosing' or sequential smaller doses of EPO. Just enough of a boost, but too small to spike/dip the data.

THE WORLD ANTI-DOPING AGENCY - WADA

WHEREABOUTS RULE

- Introduced in 2004.
- Athletes must provide to their Anti-Doping Agency (eg UK Anti-Doping) details of their location for one hour everyday between 5am & 11pm.
- 2015 - standard 2 years ban for missing 3 in 12 months.
- eg 2003 Rio Ferdinand was banned for 8 months & fined £50,000 for failing to take a test.

THE ROLE OF WADA

- Founded in 1999, an International Independent Agency, funded by the sports movement & national governments.

- WADA aims to bring consistency to anti-doping policies & regulations within sports organisations & governments worldwide. Leads a collaborative worldwide movement for 'doping free' sport.

- Plays the lead role in scientific research, education & developing anti-doping capabilities & monitoring. (World Anti-Doping Code).

- Governments, IGBs & NGBs agree to this code & sign up as signatories.

- Within WADA there is an Intelligence & Investigation Team that work with law enforcement to target & shut down large scale doping rings.

ARGUMENTS FOR / AGAINST DRUG TAKING & TESTING

- There is an ongoing debate around the use of PEDs in sport & the effectiveness of drug testing.
- Many performers, fans & pundits believe that PED use is rife in elite sport. The majority agree that performers should be clean.

FOR

- **Natural Inequalities.** Some argue that performers are born with natural advantage PED use would 'level the playing field'.

- **Fair Competition.** If PED use was legal, competition would be fair (all have access).

- **Maximising Human Potential.** PEDs can push the boundaries of athletic achievement. More exciting performances & broken records.

- **Freedom of Choice.** There should be right to choose (so long as risks are known).

- **Advancement of Technology.** Allows for faster recovery & improved performance.

- **What is a PED?** Sometimes it can be difficult to decide what is a legal supplement or process. e.g. creatine monohydrate & hypoxic tents. Both legal but give the user an (unfair) advantage.

AGAINST

- **Reduction in Fair Play.** Allowing PED use gives an unfair advantage to those that use them.

- **Inequality of Access.** Not all performers would have access to the same quality of drugs or medical advice (especially poorer nations).

- **Long term Health Risks.** The use of PEDs carries significant health risks, including CV problems, liver & kidney damage, hormone imbalances plus mental health issues such as depression & aggression.

- **Addiction & Dependence.** Some drugs can lead to addiction &/or psychological dependence & affect a performer's long term mental health & wellbeing.

- **Moral Integrity.** Many believe performers should succeed based on natural ability & hard work.

- **Negative Role Models.** It may encourage younger performers to also use PEDs.

- **Pressure.** Performers may feel pressured to take them, even if they are against drug taking.

- **Cost.** The cost & time taken for testing is very expensive & continually evolving. There is a feeling it is an 'un-winnable' scenario. (Both FOR & AGAINST)

THE ENHANCED GAMES

- The **Enhanced Games** has a commitment to provide a scientifically guided environment where performers can maximise their performance under safe conditions, by using **PEDs** under clinical supervision.

- The games give performers an informed picture of their health, including a 'state of the art' pre-competition medical screening assessment.
This helps monitor cardiac risks & other key health markers.

- All performers competing in the **Enhanced Games** will be paid, with the first performers to set World Records in the...
- 100m sprint
- 50m freestyle
will receive $1,000,000 USD!

- Doctor Aron Ping D'Souza (President of the Enhanced Games), believes in '... medical and scientific process of elevating humanity to its full potential', through a community of committed athletes.

- He and his team believe that for too long, the **Anti-Doping regime** has been marred by scandal & inefficacy, undermining the integrity of sports & betraying the trust of performers worldwide.

- eg: 23 Chinese swimmers tested positive for the heart medication Trimetazidine (increases cardiac function & enhances exercise capacity) but were cleared to compete in the **Tokyo Olympics** & won 6 medals.

- At the time of writing, the first **Enhanced Games** are scheduled for the second half of 2025. Potential host cities are currently being sounded out... www.enhanced.org.

THE USES OF SPORTS LEGISLATION

SPORT & THE LAW

- Have traditionally been considered as separate areas.

- However more recently there have been an increasing amount of lawsuits due to deviant acts or breaches of contract.

eg. Australian rugby player Israel Folau had his contract terminated with Rugby Australia in 2019 for a post on social/media regarding homosexuality & his faith.

- However Folau took legal action & an out of court settlement was agreed.

- Issues relating to violent acts are mostly dealt with by clubs or the NGB as they have their own judicial system, but sometimes violent or unlawful acts in sport can be prosecuted outside of sport.

eg. 18 yr old Ben Collett was playing for Manchester United Middlesborough in 2008, when he was tackled by Gary Smith; a tackle that was high & over the ball. As a result Collett fractured his tibia & fibula of his right leg.

- Collett pursued the club (Middlesborough), not Smith, arguing that they were liable for their employees actions, given he was connected to the club & acting in his employment as a professional footballer.

- Middlesborough admitted liability & Collett awarded £4.3 million damages.

NGBs

- Are responsible for creating the rules & regulations that govern their sport.

- These are based on a set of principles, policies & conducts that provide safety in equipment & facilities and that support the moral values of fair play & sportsmanship.

CONTRACTS

- A legally binding agreement between 2 (or more) interested parties.

- Could be performer, club, NGB, coach, sponsor.

- Player contracts focus on duration, salary, bonuses & duties.

- Performers/players are employees - they have a contract & employment rights.

- In 1995 THE BOSMAN RULING meant that players could move to a new club at the end of their contract without a fee being paid. Can now sign 'pre-contract agreements' if their current deal has less than 6 months remaining.

ELITE SPORT

- Has become more commercialised & exposed in the media, so any inappropriate behaviour is more likely to attract the attention of law enforcing agencies. Sport is seen by the law as a 'special area' where by the law & legal systems do not directly interfere with the specific rules in relation to that specific sport.

THE USES OF SPORTS LEGISLATION

- In 2013, Russian boxer Magomed Abdusalamov fought Mike Perez at Madison Square Garden in New York.

- After the bout, which he lost on points & after initial care by the ringside doctors, he was deemed fine to leave.

- He was later taken to hospital for a CT scan, where a brain bleed was found. He had multiple strokes & was left paralysed on his right side.

- Abdusalamov initially tried to sue the referee for negligence & he was paid $22 million by the state of New York. The case with the 3 doctors is still ongoing.

- Rugby referees also need to be extra vigilant, especially with the new tackle height laws & the scrum.

- There have been many cases over the years where a referee has acted in a negligent manner for not controlling the scrum after multiple collapses, leading to spinal injuries.

OFFICIALS (NEGLIGENCE)

- Negligence is defined as... 'the failure to exercise the care or duty of care towards others which a reasonable or prudent person would do in the same or similar circumstances.'

- Officials have a responsibility, or duty of care to ensure they enforce the rules or laws competently to allow not only for a fair game, but to reduce injuries so performers can compete in a safe environment.

- If officials fail to do this, they could be seen as negligent.

- For example, if a game of football was played on a frozen pitch and a player sustains an injury as a direct result.

THE USES OF SPORTS LEGISLATION

SPECTATORS (SAFETY & HOOLIGANISM)

- Sports legislation plays a crucial role managing & regulating behaviours of spectators to ensure...

- the safety of patrons, prevent violence & maintain a positive environment free of harassment & racism at sporting events.

SPECTATOR SAFETY

- Stadium Safety Regulations - Government imposed, such as fire safety, enough emergency exits & crowd control measures.

- Seating Requirement - to segregate opposing fans (football) & prevent overcrowding.

- Emergency Protocols - clear protocols in case of fire, terrorist threats or natural disasters.

- Occupier Liability Act (1957) safety & security.

- Sports Ground Safety Authority Act (2011) overseas venue safety.

COACHES (DUTY OF CARE)

- Duty of care is defined as 'a moral or legal obligation to ensure the safety or well-being of others if they are responsible for a group of people.'

- When coaches are responsible for minors (children) in a team, they are said to be in 'loco parentis', a Latin phrase referring to 'in the place of a parent.'

- A coach's responsibility is not just developing skills in a sporting environment, it also includes a wider role including wellbeing, health & safety & protection from abuse (all clubs are legally required to have a Child Protection lead).

- All coaches must have up to date DBS clearance.

- Appropriate supervision must be maintained, First Aid procedures in place & Risk Assessments.

- Example (Anderson v Lyotier) a skier who successfully sued his instructor after serious injury after following dangerous instructions.

- They went down a very steep off-piste slope with no experience at that level.

Spectator Behaviour and Hooliganism

Strategies to Combat

- Early kick offs. Games start before the pubs open!
- All seater stadia. Potential troublemakers unable to move around the crowd. Clubs have control over tickets. Decreased capacity means an increase in costs.
- Segregation of fans. Separated from opposing fans. Gap with stewards/police. Again additional cost.
- Improved security. Checks at turn-stiles, CCTV inside out, more police present, better trained stewards. CCTV police spotters with fans. CCTV can identify troublemakers. Again very costly.
- Alcohol restrictions. Early kick offs limit sales. Banned in away end (may cause trouble?) Not allowed in view of the pitch.
- Travel restrictions/banning orders. Stops known hooligans attending games. Attend police station on match day.
- Education, campaigns & high profile endorsements. Have players/role models appeal for better behaviour. 'Kick it Out' - focusses on racism.... still!

Spectator Behaviour

- Fans help create a great atmosphere. eg - midweek European Cup matches - noise, chanting, singing.
- Gives the home team an advantage - support. (Home field)
- Boo, whistle & jeer opposition. Intimidating & can inhibit performance.

However, they can also have a negative effect......

- on performance as a result of increased pressure. Causes ↑ anxiety levels to ↑ & performance.

- Potential for crowd trouble/hooliganism - inside/outside ground.

- this can lead to safety concerns. stewards, police & CCTV all costly. Games/events are assessed to manage potential risk of trouble. Cost of repairs if ground damaged eg - seats ripped out.

- Potential negative effect on part-icipation numbers amongst younger performers. Violence at games may lead to younger fans losing interest & playing the sport.

Good spectator behaviour or etiquette means watching & behaving in a respectful manner. eg - being quiet during the opposing national anthem, being quiet during rallies in tennis, place kicks in rugby & tee shots in golf.

Reasons why......

- historic, local derbies (no love lost). Rivalries.
- hype - big match, final?
- alcohol/drugs - stereo-typical image. Hooligan fuelled by booze. Think invincible!
- gang culture. Pack mentality. Tribal. Want to protect their area. Stand their ground.

COMMERCIALISATION, SPONSORSHIP AND THE MEDIA

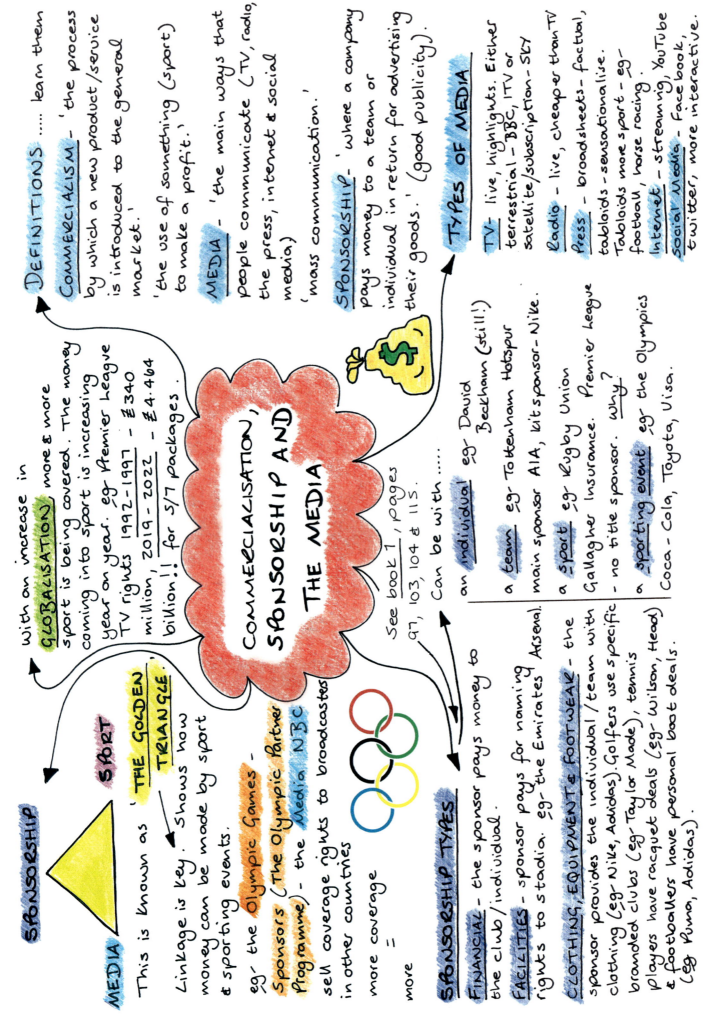

DEFINITIONS ..... learn them

COMMERCIALISM - 'the process by which a new product/service is introduced to the general market.'

'the use of something (sport) to make a profit.'

MEDIA - 'the main ways that people communicate (TV, radio, the press, internet & social media)

'mass communication.'

SPONSORSHIP - 'where a company pays money to a team or individual in return for advertising their goods.' (good publicity).

TYPES OF MEDIA

<u>TV</u> - live, highlights. Either terrestrial - BBC, ITV or satellite/subscription - SKY

<u>Radio</u> - live, cheaper than TV

<u>Press</u> - broadsheets - factual, tabloids - sensationalise. Tabloids more sport - eg - football, horse racing.

<u>Internet</u> - streaming, YouTube

<u>Social Media</u> - Facebook, twitter, more interactive.

SPONSORSHIP

MEDIA

This is known as 'THE GOLDEN TRIANGLE'

Linkage is key. Shows how money can be made by sport & sporting events.

eg - the Olympic Games - Sponsors (The Olympic Partner Programme) - the Media NBC sell coverage rights to broadcasters in other countries = more coverage

with an increase in GLOBALISATION more & more sport is being covered. The money coming into sport is increasing year on year. eg - Premier League TV rights 1992-1997 - £340 million. 2019-2022 - £4.464 billion!! for 5/7 packages.

See book 1, pages 97, 103, 104 & 115.

Can be with .....

an <u>individual</u> eg - David Beckham (still!)

a <u>team</u> eg - Tottenham Hotspur main sponsor AIA, kit sponsor - Nike.

a <u>sport</u> eg - Rugby Union Gallagher Insurance. Premier League - no title sponsor. why?

a <u>sporting event</u> eg - the Olympics Coca-Cola, Toyota, Visa.

SPONSORSHIP TYPES

<u>FINANCIAL</u> - the sponsor pays money to the club/individual.

<u>FACILITIES</u> - sponsor pays for naming rights to stadia. eg - the Emirates (Arsenal).

<u>CLOTHING, EQUIPMENT & FOOTWEAR</u> - the sponsor provides the individual/team with clothing (eg - Nike, Adidas). Golfers use specific branded clubs (eg - TaylorMade), tennis players have racquet deals (eg - Wilson, Head) & footballers have personal boot deals. (eg - Puma, Adidas).

THE POSITIVE IMPACT OF COMMERCIALISATION, SPONSORSHIP & THE MEDIA

COACH

- Increased profile.
- Higher salaries.
- Increased technology used to analyse the opposition.

SPORT

- Increase in the amount of income for the sport.
- Results in more income for grass roots initiatives.
- Increased media coverage & sponsorship.
- More professional structure for leagues, coaching, officiating & play as pathways.
- Improved facilities (training, playing & for the spectator).

PERFORMERS

- Higher salaries, so can train & play full time.
- Increased talent ID & pathways for performers to progress.
- Sport for elite performers eg. UK sport world class programme.
- Celebrity status if successful.
- Greater access to higher quality coaching & training facilities.

OFFICIAL

- More investment into training to create better adjudication of play.
- The role becomes professional; now able to due full time as a career.
- Celebrity profile from officiating important & televised games (a good thing?).

AUDIENCE

- Better viewing as the standards of performances have increased.
- Stadium facilities have improved as new stadia built.
- Greater access to watch all events on multiple sports channels (sky, TNT, Prime et).
- Elite events have increased entertainment pre, during & post event. eg. bands, cheerleaders, competitions and free merchandise.

THE NEGATIVE IMPACT OF COMMERCIALISATION, SPONSORSHIP & THE MEDIA

SPORT

- Media plays a role in increasing pressure on the coach.
- TV companies & sponsors can dictate kick off times & time outs (especially in the US)
- Media will play more lucrative sports (eg football) that have larger audiences. Lesser known/minority sports suffer as a result.
- Sponsors can dictate elements of a performer's behaviours & appearance. eg. must wear their branded gear at all times.

- Can be very expensive to watch at the venue & at home.
- Lesser known/minority sports get little coverage.
- Advert breaks have increased due to the influence of sponsors promoting/advertising their product.

COACH

- Intense pressure to deliver results. Often coach/manager sacked due to poor performances.
- Sometimes they do not have full control of the team. General Managers, CEOs make decisions based on finances, TV deals, sponsorship etc.

- Media highlight mistakes, putting greater pressure on officials (& risk of demotion to lower leagues).

AUDIENCE

- Traditions of some sports have decreased to speed up the game. More focus on the 'global approach' rather than nurturing the 'home-grown' element.

PERFORMERS

- Increased pressure to win, gain success, renew contracts & sponsorship deals (win at all costs).
- Increased incidences of deviant behaviour (due to above).
- Unstable market due to performers being treated as commodities. eg. sold/traded.
- Sponsors can be demanding on the performer & expect certain appearances & wear certain clothing & specific behaviours.

OFFICIAL

- Increased pressure due to the money involved in sport, plus increased technology eg. TMO, VAR.
- Too dependent on technology (headsets, VAR etc.). Not available at lower levels. Standards of officiating can decrease.

IN

UNDERSTANDING OF TECHNOLOGY FOR SPORTS ANALYTICS

QUANTITATIVE DATA

- Refers to numerical measurable data that is objective & used when analysing statistics.
- Includes performance metrics, such as speed, distance, force, heart rate.
- In fitness testing, quantitative data can be obtained through a gas analysis test (respiratory values recorded).

QUALITATIVE DATA

- Includes non-numerical insights, opinions & feelings about a performance that is subjective eg judges opinions about a dance.
- Both quantitative and qualitative data can and should be used together when evaluating a performance.

USE OF TECHNOLOGY

- The use of technology in data collection focusses on...
  - SUBJECTIVE
  - VALIDITY
  - RELIABILITY
  - QUANTITATIVE
  - QUALITATIVE
  - OBJECTIVE
  (more on pages 13-14)

Table

TECHNOLOGY

- TECHNOLOGY has revolutionised the sports industry it is ever developing & changing.
- A massive change has been seen in the way performers prepare, perform & recover from activities & training.
- Specialist roles have been created alongside the coaching team, such as sports analysts & biomechanists.

Pre Mid Post

SPORTS ANALYTICS

- Refers to using data to assist teams and performers to achieve their optimum & help to improve training & performance strategies.
- The data can also be used to create mathematical models that predict various outcomes. eg opposition weaknesses.

- eg GPS data gives an understanding of work rate & distance covered (quantitative) & video analysis focusses on positioning & decision making in key moments (qualitative). Allows a more holistic approach.

UNDERSTANDING OF TECHNOLOGY FOR SPORTS ANALYTICS II

VALIDITY

- Refers to data that is purely based on facts & measurements that have very little human interpretation.
- eg. time taken to complete the 100m freestyle in swimming can be used to make an objective assessment of performance.

OBJECTIVE

- For quantitative data to be valid, it must measure what it is intended/meant to measure.
- In fitness testing, the 'tester' must determine whether the test evaluates the C.o.f chosen.

- eg. the Multi-stage fitness test does try to correlate the different levels of predicted VO₂ max. However, there is greater validity & reliability with using gas analysis, heart rate data & blood samples to determine VO₂ max in a laboratory.

SUBJECTIVE

- Data derived from coach or scout observations.

- eg. a performer may use the Borg Scale (or RPE) to assess the level of intensity during a VO₂ max test, based on their feelings & opinions.

RELIABILITY

- Refers to whether the results are consistent & can be reproduced over time.
- More on factors to consider on page 14.
- Technologies such as force plates & heart rate monitors (which are less influenced by external factors), generally offer higher reliability.

- However, equipment malfunctions & equipment that hasn't been calibrated correctly, or improper use, can reduce reliability.

- Timing gates or touch pads in swimming (when calibrated correctly) offer high validity for tracking as opposed to a stopwatch.

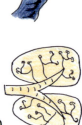

152

VIDEO & ANALYSIS PROGRAMMES

DIGITAL TECHNOLOGY

- Is used by sports analysts, coaches & performers to not only collect performance data, but to analyse biomechanical aspects & technique issues of a performance, application of tactics & behavioural elements (i.e. how performers react & position themselves in high stakes situations).

- Technological software such as Dartfish is used by coaches (& performers) to view & analyse performances, as well as editing to compare technique & biomechanical movements, to others.

- eg teaching or attempting to correct a gymnast's technique in a certain skill, such as a somersault.

OPTA SPORTS

- Is a British sports analytics company that provides data (collected & delivered in real time), by expert analysts & enriched with computer vision & AI.

- This way, the system can supply more player & team statistics, for more games, at a faster rate that is accurate.

- It can also generate in-depth & detailed performance & tracking data for historical fixtures, allowing players & coaches to plan tactics accordingly.

PERFORMANCE ANALYSIS

- Involves observations to enhance performance & improve decision making, primarily delivered through objective statistical data (data analysis) & visual feedback (video analysis).

- Research shows that on average coaches & performers only recall 30% of performance accurately/correctly.

- Performance Analysis helps with the remaining 70% by providing the facts of what happened.

- The UKSI Performance Analysis team work closely with coaches & performers to provide relevant key information (objective). This allows for evidence based decisions & reduces inaccurate subjective ones.

153

TESTING & RECORDING EQUIPMENT

CARBON DIOXIDE PRODUCTION

- Records the amount of carbon dioxide exhaled. This helps assess the metabolic fuel being used (fat vs carbohydrate) & energy expenditure overall. (VCO_2).

RESPIRATORY EXCHANGE RATIO

- The ratio of VCO_2 to VO_2 provides valuable information into what fuel (fats or carbohydrates) the body is primarily using during exercise. (RER)

RESTING METABOLIC RATE

- Can be used to measure the energy the body expends at rest. This can assist in implementing an appropriate nutritional plan. (RMR)

KEY FUNCTIONALITY

OXYGEN CONSUMPTION

- Measures the amount of oxygen consumed (maximum oxygen uptake). A key indicator of aerobic capacity. (VO_2)

VALIDITY AND RELIABILITY ISSUES

Calibration - done regularly to maintain accuracy.

Expertise - reliability depends on the expertise of the 'tester'.

Cost - the equipment is quite expensive.

Demanding - the test procedures are quite demanding (often maximal) & so not suitable for all clients.

METABOLIC CART

- Is a device used to measure a person's metabolic rate through indirect calorimetry.

INDIRECT CALORIMETRY

- Calculates energy expenditure by measuring the amount of oxygen consumed (VO_2) & carbon dioxide (VCO_2) produced during respiration.

- These measurements can provide information into how the body uses energy during exercise & energy during exercise & at rest.

GPS & MOTION TRACKING

TRACKMAN

- The trackman machine is becoming increasingly popular in golf, where it can track a shot from 6 foot pitches to 400 yard drives, pinpointing the landing position with an accuracy of less than 1 foot at 100 yards. The shots can be presented in 3D, illustrating the trajectory as well as other parameters in real time (data can be delivered to electronic devices such as an iPad within a second).

- Examples of key parameters include... swing technique, launch angle, smash factor, ball speed, club head speed, attack angle & club path.

ADIDAS GMR INSOLES

- This smart insole can track the players' running speed, the power of the kick, touch & control/distance run by the player & the ability to pass the football

- It is motorised by a Jacquard chip (Google) placed inside the insole of the football boot.

FITNESS TRACKERS

- Heart rate monitors & pedometers are still used, though the evolution of fitness tracker & smart wrist bands have combined both & added extra data.

- These devices track HR (though some have stopped this on newer versions to save battery) & also track distance, calories used, steps & monitor sleep.

GLOBAL POSITIONING SYSTEM - GPS

- Commonly used by elite athletes in team sports during matches & in training. The performance analyst uses the stats to feedback to the strength & conditioning coach. Stats included are... metres covered, top sprint speed & heart rate data.

- Data is used to manage player workload & developing areas of weakness.

- Coaches are able to establish player physiological limitations & use the data for basis of making tactical changes during games as stats are now available concurrently.

- More affordable GPS units are now available & are being developed at a foot pace. These can be purchased via the use of a smart watch & can be used for various sports, both on land & in water. eg. Skagen Falster 3.

BAT SENSOR

- Bat sensors (Intel-powered Specular or Stancebeam) can be placed at the top of the bat & can measure key elements such as... back lift angle, follow through angle, impact angle, maximum bat speed, bat speed at impact, time to impact, 3D swing & plane path.

- Used to calculate shot timing efficiency & correlate data with Hawk Eye to see how effective the shot is & how it can be improved.

There are many! Examples here include...

155

DATA INTEGRITY

- Maintaining data integrity refers to ensuring that all data entered into the 'system' is done correctly, with the view that it can be retrieved in the same format at a later date, if this data is required/needed.

- There are some general rules to follow to ensure data integrity...

- Adherence to General Data Protection Regulation (GDPR).

- This act came into force in 2018 & requires everyone responsible for using personal data to follow strict rules.

Like all industries, sport has become increasingly digitised, with technology being used to improve engagement with the fan base through social media, to sell tickets & to provide team news & updates.

MAINTAINING DATA INTEGRITY

- Sports organisations hold large amounts of personal data eg: medical records, sponsorship deals, contact details & salaries.

- This information can become valuable to online attackers, which can lead to cyber-attacks that demand a ransom for the data to be returned. Online attackers can look to target high net worth individuals & use sensitive information as blackmail.

- To maintain the integrity of data, there should be...
- Password secure files.
- Security software
- A backing up of data regularly.
- Software that only allows relevant data to be entered & saved.

Information should be used...
- fairly
- lawfully
- transparently

FUNCTIONS OF SPORTS ANALYTICS

FUNCTIONS

- Sports Analytics has become an integral part of modern sport, to assist all aspects of performance, including...

GAME ANALYSIS

- Performance data collects stats on players actions.
  - eg. passes, shots, tackles etc & team movements eg. space coverage, possession, formations to inform future changes to strategy & tactics.
- Informs coaching decisions with objective data, allowing for strategic in-game adjustments & substitutions
  - GPS data can indicate that the performer has played to their limits.
- Advanced metrics (Player efficiency ratings) provide deeper insights into performance levels.

SKILLS & TECHNIQUE DEVELOPMENT

- Identify areas of weakness - give feedback.
- Help review performance to correct weakness.
- Biomechanical tools eg. force plates can help improve performance.

MONITOR FITNESS FOR PERFORMANCE

- Wearable technology (eg GPS, HR monitors) use certain metrics such as distance covered, speed, calories & workload to assess fitness.
- This helps performers optimise their training programmes based on data collected.

INJURY PREVENTION

- Helps predict & prevent injuries by analysing workload & physiological stressors.
- GPS helps to monitor workload & the data can be used to monitor potential overtraining
- Vibration technology can help promote proprioceptive function, reducing muscle tension.
- Electrostimulation can also provide benefits, such as helping repair micro-tears & strengthening muscle tissue to mimic the neuromuscular activity to allow muscles to contract & relax.

TALENT IDENTIFICATION & SCOUTING

- Helps scouts make data driven decisions.
- Help to assess potential talent.
- Predictive Modelling to predict the potential & likelihood of future success.
- Allows for efficient comparisons eg. age, levels, leagues etc.

WEARABLE TECHNOLOGY

WEARABLE TECH

- Has become increasingly popular in recent years & has been available since the mid 2000's.

- Aim ... to provide innovative ways to address physical inactivity issues & increasing sedentary lifestyles that have become part & parcel of modern day life (sadly!)

- Wearable technology such as...
  - smartphones
  - smart watches
  - wristbands
  - GPS devices

are self tracking tools that are capable of monitoring heart rate, weight, intensity levels, movement patterns, sleep, diet & emotions.

- According to a survey by Attest in 2019, 37.6% of 'millenials' own a smart watch with a health tracker.

- Statista state that the number of wearable devices worldwide more than doubled between 2016 & 2019 from 325 million to 722 million, with a forecast of more than 1 billion by 2022.

As with most things, there are Pros & Cons associated with wearable technology. Most tech is very expensive & once you rely on the data it produces, it is hard to do without.

BENEFITS

- Provides people with the ability to track & monitor fitness levels, location & movement intensity with GPS.

- Most of the devices are 'hands free' & portable

- 'Wearables' are connected to smart devices transmitting this information to them to view in real time &/or later.

- Can help people set goals & take more responsibility in tracking health & progress (rather than relying on someone else).

DRAWBACKS

- Short battery life, some function may not work to save battery life. eg Apple watches have a shorter battery life than a fit-bit tracker.

- Reports of inaccurate data being measured & inconsistencies between different devices/apps (eg Strava & Nike Run Club). Could be dangerous if tracking HR for a heart condition.

- No conclusive evidence that the rise has increased participation rate.

- Cost. £ $ #

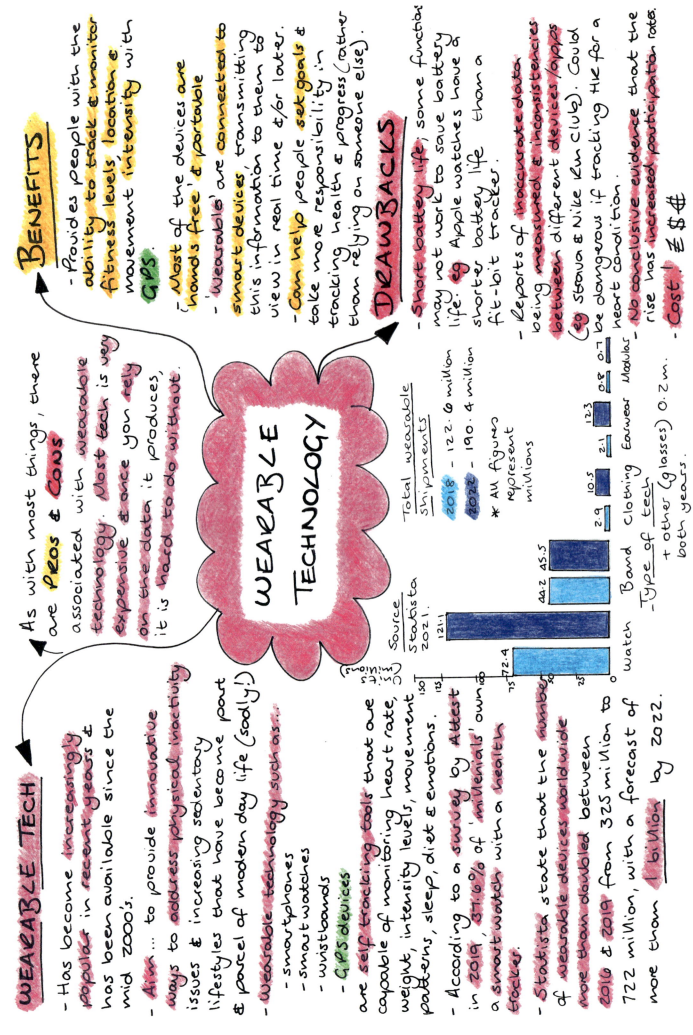

Total wearable shipments

- 2018 — 122.6 million
- 2022 — 190.4 million

* All figures represent millions

Source Statista 2021.

Type of tech
+ other (glasses) 0.2 m in both years.

Watch | Band | Clothing | Earwear Modules
72.4 | 2.9 | 10.5 | 2.1 | 12.3
121.1 | 44.2 | 45.5 | 0.8 | 0.7

THE IMPACT OF MATERIAL TECHNOLOGY ON EQUIPMENT

ASSISTIVE TECHNOLOGY
(VISUALLY IMPAIRED)

- Devices like beeping balls (for goalball).
- Enables visually impaired performers to take part in competitive sports with improved sensory feedback & awareness.

PROSTHETICS
(RUNNING)

- Carbon fibre prosthetics/blades are lightweight & highly flexible. They mimic the natural elasticity of tendons for energy efficient running.

TECHNOLOGICAL ADVANCEMENTS

- Have narrowed the gap between able bodied, disabled & aging performers in the 21st century.
- Disabled performers rely on specialised equipment to participate in sports.
- Advances in technology have made the equipment lighter, stronger & more customised, enhancing performance.
- Here are some examples...

WHEELCHAIRS
(WHEELCHAIR SPORTS)

- Racing & sport specific models are constructed with lightweight materials such as aluminium, carbon fibre & titanium. These offer high strength to weight ratios, making the equipment durable & reducing its weight.
- Lighter, more manoeuvrable wheelchairs allow performers move faster with greater agility.

LIGHTER RACQUETS, CLUBS & BATS

- Carbon fibre, graphite & composite materials are now used in tennis racquets, golf clubs, cricket & baseball bats to make them lighter while retaining strength & durability.
- Lighter equipment reduces strain physical on older performers, allowing them to maintain power & precision without over exertion.

CUSHIONED & SUPPORTIVE FOOTWEAR

- Modern running shoes now include high tech foam, gel & air cushioning to offer support & absorption (for older performers).
- This improves comfort & decreases the risk of injury. eg. joint issues.

FACILITIES – OLYMPIC LEGACY

VENUES

- Permanent venues post London 2012 have all been **successfully reopened as public amenities**, such as the Aquatics Centre, Lee Valley Velo Park & the Copper Box (a multi-sport venue).

OLYMPIC STADIUM

- Is now the permanent home of West Ham United football club. The club moved to the stadium in 2016 from the Boleyn Ground at Upton Park on a **99** year lease.
- It cost a further **£323** million to convert the stadium **to a multi-purpose venue**.
- The London stadium also hosts athletics events, concerts & other sports, such as rugby union, rugby league & baseball.

FUNDING

- For **Places & Spaces** came from a **£7 million** National Lottery funding pot, where awards of ~10,000 can be given to create/improve local facilities.

- Sport England in partnership with the **British Olympic** Association, the **British Paralympic** Association & support from the London Organising Committee of the Olympic Games on the back of the **London Games of 2012** started an initiative called **'Places, People, Play'**.

- This was a **£135 million** initiative that was divided into **9** separate schemes to help **improve facilities** in local communities.

3G PITCHES

- There has been a **rise in these pitches over the past** 15-20 years. 3G pitches are flexible, durable & can operate all year, with significant usage from informal recreational activity, to training & match play.

PLACES & SPACES

- Was an initiative set up as part of the **Birmingham 2022** Commonwealth Games to help community sport & physical activity groups **improve places & spaces** across the country.

TECHNOLOGY IN SPORT

TECHNOLOGY for a performe can also help to...

LOWER THE RISK OF INJURY
- Researches/technology specialists are developing ever changing tech to make sport safer, including...
- **HELMETS** in high contact sports eg American football that release air as a 'shock absorber' when there is an impact.
- **MOUTHGUARDS** with LED lights that monitor & assess impact that may lead to a concussion. 'Low' impact - blue light 'Devastating' impact - red
- Plus 'basic' safety equipment such as shinpads, appropriate footwear for running, football etc.

QUICKER RECOVERY FROM INJURY
- Huge recent advances here. See Contemporary Recovery Methods on page 166.

Can have both **POSITIVE** & **NEGATIVE** impacts on...
- the **PERFORMER**
- the **SPORT**
- **OFFICIALS**
- **SPECTATORS**
- **COACHES**

THE PERFORMER
- Uses technology to **ENHANCE PERFORMANCE.**
- There are lots of examples here.

METHODS - can be linked to tracking heart rates (via monitors), running stats (GPS), nutritional analysis to name but a few. More on page 158. Many of these are wearable tech.

EQUIPMENT - Lighter, bigger, stronger cricket bats, tennis racquets & golf clubs allow balls to be hit harder (sometimes further) & with more control. Ultra light weight carbon fibre cycles/bikes. eg. The Ineos Grenadiers' Tour de France 2022 bike (the Pinarello Dogma F12) weighs just 6.8 kg & costs £12,700!!

CLOTHING - Base layers, full body swimsuits for swimmers/triathletes, all in one cycling suits, running shoes with carbon fibre plates eg Nike Vaporfly (now banned by World Athletics), light weight football boots, tight fitting clothing in rugby & body armour for protection.

DISABLED ATHLETES
- There have been huge advances in tech for 'Para Sport' over the past 10-15 years, including...
- Carbon fibre running blades.
- Badminton chairs.
- Modified track cycling bikes.
- Release braces for archery.
- Tapping devices for swimmers
- Wheelchair racing chairs & gloves.

TECHNOLOGY IN SPORT

OFFICIALS DECISIONS INFLUENCED BY TECHNOLOGY

- Officials, especially in football now seem to 'bottle' making big decisions.
- They seem to have become reliant / over reliant on video replays.
- Gets rid of the human error' aspect. Is this good or bad?
- Can be vilified or victimised if they get big decisions wrong.
- The impact of all these checks is that there is a

POTENTIAL REDUCTION IN THE FLOW OF THE GAME

- As technology increases & more & more checks take place, this is becoming more of an issue.
- An increased number of stoppages in football to check for offsides & penalties.
- Rugby matches (80 mins) taking over 100 mins due to repeated TMO checks such as the grounding of the ball for a try.

HOWEVER...

- Not all the impacts of technology on officiating are positive.
- The officials may delay/ alter their decisions (referring to video replays - often in slow-mo) & this reduces the flow of the game.

OFFICIALS

- Much more work has been done recently to help officials in terms of technology.
- Main reasons...

TO INCREASE FAIR PLAY & INCREASE ACCURACY OF OFFICIATING.

- A lot of pressure on officials to make the correct decision.
Why? Results ultimately mean $£!!
eg's include...
Hawk Eye - Ball tracking used in tennis, cricket & football.
TMO - Television Match Official in rugby union & league
VAR - Video Assistant Referee in football.
(More on page 163).

MORE ACCURATE DECISIONS

- The use of tech should allow officials to make more accurate decisions & it can be beneficial if used correctly/well.
- However, as can be seen in the Premier League (football) this is not always the case.

- The use of technology 'on the field of play' can also be used by performers if they disagree with a decision by an official.
Examples include...
Cricket - a player can review a decision if given out/not out.
Tennis a player can review a decision if the ball is deemed out.

TECHNOLOGY IN SPORT

AT HOME
- The main positives here concern the quality of coverage & the amount/range of games & sports covered.
- Ever improving technology is bringing the audience at home 'ever closer' to the action!

- Games/events can be seen in HD, 4k, 3D and interactively (Red Button).
- There are more games covered, more camera angles, cameras on players (Cricket - the Hundred), cameras on officials (rugby) & on equipment (Cricket - stumps, football goals).
- A huge amount of choice with different channels & broadcasters.
- The internet allows for games/events to be streamed & mobile apps such as 'Sky Go' allow sport to be viewed 'On the go'!
- Events can be watched from the comfort of your own home.
- Changes to fixture times, days & even seasons (Rugby League) for TV.
- Stop start nature of games now due to VAR, TMO etc.

SPECTATORSHIP
in sport has been hugely impacted by technology.
- Sport can be viewed...
- LIVE in the stadium
- AT HOME watching on TV.

LIVE
- If you watch games live at the ground, in some sports (eg rugby) you may see replays & reviews of major incidents, such as a review of a high tackle or the grounding of the ball for a try.
- Replays of VAR decisions tend not to happen in football, hence why fans at games do not like it, as they are left 'in the dark' over decisions.
- Some stadia have very large screens, such as the Alexander stadium, venue for the athletics events for the 2022 Commonwealth Games. Here fans could see close up footage of events in 'real time' & 'slow-mo'.

HOWEVER... it is not all positive!
- It can be very very expensive to watch a range of sports via different broadcasters eg. sky, Amazon Prime.
- May need specialist equipment.
- 'Amateur' fans may affect numbers at live venues - decrease in revenue for clubs.
- Fibre optic broadband not available everywhere - may be needed for high quality streaming.

Virgin media

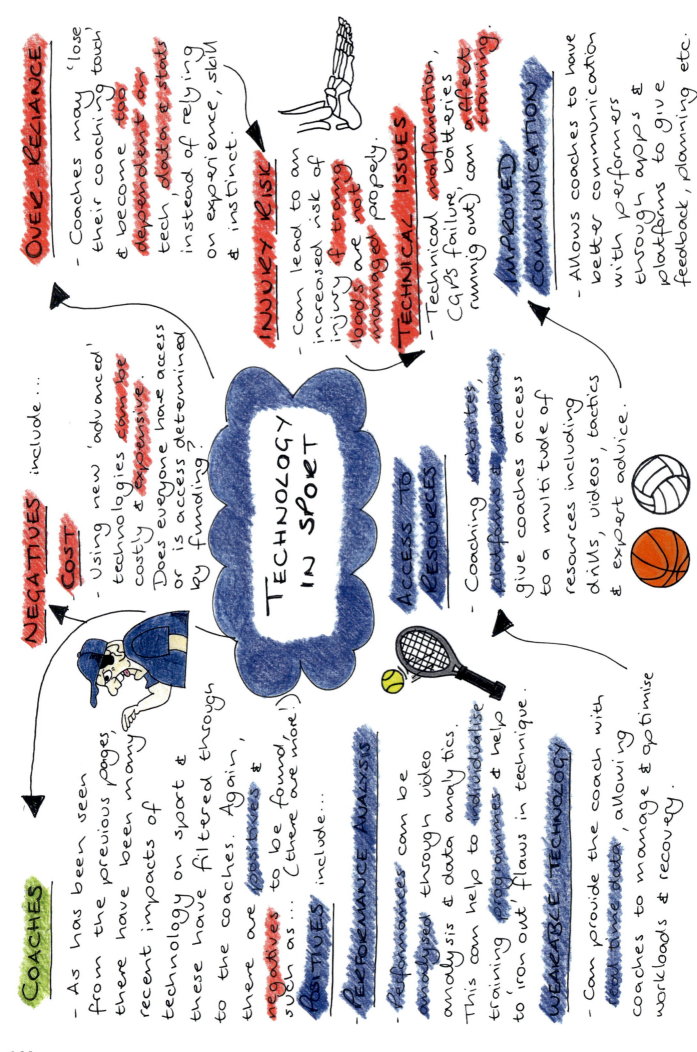

TECHNOLOGY IN SPORT

OVER-RELIANCE

- Coaches may 'lose their coaching touch' & become too dependent on tech, data & stats instead of relying on experience, skill & instinct.

INJURY RISK

- Can lead to an increased risk of injury if training loads are not managed properly.

TECHNICAL ISSUES

- Technical malfunction, (GPS failure, batteries running out) can affect training.

IMPROVED COMMUNICATION

- Allows coaches to have better communication with performers through apps & platforms to give feedback, planning etc.

NEGATIVES include...

COST

- Using new 'advanced' technologies can be costly & expensive. Does everyone have access or is access determined by funding?

COACHES

- As has been seen from the previous pages, there have been many recent impacts of technology on sport & these have filtered through to the coaches. Again, there are positives & negatives to be found (there are more!) such as...

POSITIVES include...

PERFORMANCE ANALYSIS

- Performances can be analysed through video analysis & data analytics. This can help to individualise training programmes & help to 'iron out' flaws in technique.

WEARABLE TECHNOLOGY

- Can provide the coach with real-time data, allowing coaches to manage & optimise workloads & recovery.

ACCESS TO RESOURCES

- Coaching websites, platforms & webinars give coaches access to a multitude of resources including drills, videos, tactics & expert advice.

TECHNOLOGY IN SPORT

INCREASED COST

of technological advances

- As tech gets more cutting edge, inevitably the cost increases.
- This may mean that not all teams/performers can afford this & so in effect you get an 'uneven' playing field.
- Much of this increase in cost may be covered by sponsors.
- eg - Eliud Kipchoge running a sub 2 hour marathon, sponsored by Ineos. Retro-chemicals in Nike Vapofly Next %.

He ran on a specifically chosen course with banked turns, with the help of 41 pace runners. They ran in 5s in a Y shape & followed a laserbeam for the 'ideal' path.

Result - Kipchoge ran 26.2 miles in 1:59.40.2 in Vienna on October 12 2019.

Known as the Ineos 1.59 challenge. All paid by sponsors!

AVAILABILITY & AFFORDABILITY

of technology.

- This is directly linked to costs.
- Developing 'cutting edge' technology is getting more & more expensive.

- As has been seen, there are many, many positive impacts of technology on sport & the performer.
- HOWEVER, as has already been said, there are negative impacts too.
- These mainly centre around unequal access, cost and availability & affordability.

UNEQUAL ACCESS

to the same quality of technology.

- Not all performers will have equal access to the same technology.
- Much will depend on the 'R&D' budget - 'Research & Development' of the team or country.
- Access may depend on location also. Are you near a certain facility?
- It is estimated that Nike have spent over $5 billion on research since 2005.
- This will have a direct positive impact on athletes that are sponsored by Nike.

- As costs increase, not everyone can afford it.
- This leads to... unequal access.
- This means that increased costs, availability, affordability & unequal access are all linked.
- eg) a Hyperbaric Chamber costs up to £29,500 to buy & may cost £30 per hour long session.
- In addition to the cost, there may be limited availability in certain areas/countries.

CONTEMPORARY RECOVERY METHODS

HYPERBARIC CHAMBERS

- Hyperbaric therapy is a treatment where 100% O2 is administered under pressure greater than the atmospheric pressure.
- This accelerates the recovery of soft tissue micro-tears.

COMPRESSION CLOTHING

- Increases blood flow to muscles & increases venous return to disperse waste products eg lactic acid.

HYDROTHERAPY

- Cold water therapy has been proven to reduce muscle soreness & improve recovery times.

OXYGEN TENT

- Similar to hyperbaric chambers however O2 tents refer more 'to supplemental O2 found at normal atmospheric pressure.

CONTRAST THERAPY

- Hot/cold immersion therapy, placing a limb in warm water, followed by ice cold water. Leaves swelling

CRYOTHERAPY

- Involves exposing the body to extremely low temperatures for between 2-4 mins.
- As with ice baths, blood vessels constrict then dilate afterwards, flushing waste products from the body.

MASSAGE (PHYSIO)

- Widely used as a recovery strategy to reduce muscle soreness & stimulate blood flow.
- Beneficial for prevention & management of injury.

HYPOXIC TENTS

- Try to simulate high altitude conditions, without having to travel.
- Aims to increase EPO levels/ production (see REDs).

ICE BATHS

- Decreases/reduces inflammation & increases recovery rates.
- Blood vessels constrict, then dilate when an athlete gets out.
- Flushes out metabolic waste.

ULTRASOUND

- Ultrasound waves cause vibration of the tissue (especially those containing collagen).
- Increases muscle temperature, reduces pain & muscle spasms.
- Promotes healing process & blood flow.

- The following contemporary recovery methods allow for quicker recovery from injury.
- This is a very fluid & ever changing area, with 'new' methods being found & used all the time. Keep your eyes open for changes!

3.2.4 Sport and society and the role of technology in physical activity and sport

1. **Outline** the stages of the Sporting Development Continuum.

   (4 marks)

2. **Describe** the difference between physical education and sport.

   (2 marks)

3. **Evaluate** the role UK Sport has in developing elite talent in sport.

   (8 marks)

4. **Describe** the difference between sportsmanship to gamesmanship.

   (2 marks)

5. **Discuss** the view that all elite performers or teams should have a 'win at all costs' approach to competition.

   (8 marks)

6. Using examples, **explain** the difference between positive and negative deviance.

   (4 marks)

7. **Identify** strategies to prevent spectator violence in the sport.

   (4 marks)

8. **Examine** reasons why elite athletes would use performance enhancing drugs or methods?

   (8 marks)

9. **Explain** the physiological benefits for a Tour de France cyclist using EPO to enhance performance.

   (4 marks)

10. Dr Aron Ping D'Souza, President of the Enhanced Games believes that the anti-doping regime around the world has undermined the integrity of elite sport with their inefficiency and has pressed for an 'enhanced games' where PEDs are allowed.

Discuss the view that enhanced games will be beneficial to promote global games.   (8 marks)

11. Explain how officials in sport can be deemed to be negligent?   (4 marks)

12. Identify strategies authorities can implement to reduce the incidence of hooliganism in sport.   (4 marks)

13. Discuss the impact of commercialisation on sport.   (8 marks)

14. Describe the difference between quantitative and qualitative data.   (2 marks)

15. Define indirect calorimetry.   (1 mark)

16. Outline how data integrity can be maintained.   (3 marks)

17. Evaluate the impact of the development of equipment and facilities improves the standard of sport.   (8 marks)

Total marks   /82